The Binman's Guide to Marketing

Top 100 marketing inspirations & ideas from branding, social media, PR and digital marketing to traditional media that will increase your sales

Oisín Browne

@binmansguide

The Binman's Guide to Marketing: *Top 100 marketing inspirations & ideas from branding, social media, PR and digital marketing to traditional media that will increase your sales*

This edition is published by Drop The Monkey Publishing.
For further information: www.dropthemonkey.com

Printed in Ireland by Gemini International
Cover Design by Links Associates
Edited by TheDocCheck.Com

First Edition

ISBN 978-0-9570130-2-5

A catalogue record for this book is available from the British Library.

This publication is designed to provide accurate and authoritative information in regard to the subject matter covered. It is sold with the understanding that the publisher is not engaged in rendering legal services or other professional services. If legal advice or other expert assistance is required, the services of a competent professional person should be sought.

The author and publisher state that all writings in this book are the suggestions and views of the author and accept no responsibility for the outcome of any suggestions applied.

To buy **The Binman's Guide To Marketing** or **The Binman's Guide to Selling** in bulk contact the publisher at info@dropthemonkey.com - The book is ideal for your management team or as a corporate gift for your clients, suppliers or partners. Special discounts are available on quantity purchases by corporations, associations, businesses, networking groups, universities, business schools, sales teams, agencies, and for seminars.

Praise for The Binman's Guide to Marketing

"In The Binman's Guide to Marketing, Oisin masters the art of making the complex world of marketing simple. What else could you expect from a Binman who doesn't like to waste words. A great read!" **Gijs van Wulfen, Founder of the FORTH Innovation Method, Top 40 Innovation Blogger, and the author of the bestseller The Innovation Expedition**

"A refreshing read, packed with enthusiasm and inspiration. Who would have ever guessed a marketing book could be so cool? If your bottom line depends on great marketing, Oisin's book is your source." **Mike Michalowicz, author of Profit First, The Pumpkin Plan & The Toilet Paper Entrepreneur**

"If you want a dry and boring marketing book written by an academic don't buy this! Oisin's real world examples of success work and he uses the ideas himself. Inspirational!" **David Meerman Scott, bestselling author of The New Rules of Marketing and PR**

"Oisin's book lays out an awesome assortment of the best ideas, inspirations and interviews in marketing. This collection is a must read for any business owner or marketing executive. If you want to understand how to creatively use marketing to drive sales, this book is for you." **Alexandra Watkins, Best-selling author of Hello, My Name is Awesome: How to Create Brand Names That Stick, an Inc. Magazine Top 10 Marketing Book**

"If you want to make a mark in the world of business, read The Binman's Guide to Marketing, a terrific compilation of distilled marketing wisdom. Just a page a day, and you will toss your competition away." **Whitney Johnson, Author of Disrupt Yourself ®: Putting the Power of Disruptive Innovation to Work**

"Wow, this book is simply amazing! This is an extremely powerful marketing guide that does an incredible job of highlighting specific marketing practices and how they impact your business. It's a must read!" **Kim Garst, best selling author of Will the Real You Please Stand Up; Show Up, Be Authentic and Prosper in Social Media**

"This valuable book is the most practical and comprehensive guide to marketing I've ever read. It covers every facet of marketing and is a must-read for new marketing hires and business owners alike." **Mandy McEwen, Digital Marketing Consultant & Founder of Mod Girl Marketing**

"Any business owner is bound to find something useful in The Binman's Guide to Marketing. At the very least its comprehensive nature shows that you must dedicate time and resources to be an effective marketer." **Kevin Daum, Inc.com Columnist, best selling author of ROAR! Get Heard in the Sales and Marketing Jungle, and Video Marketing For Dummies**

"Oisin takes the fields of sales and marketing, which can be overwhelming for many people and breaks them down into simple, easy-to-understand, bite-size pieces. Inch by inch, anything's a cinch. Study one or two of Oisin's tips per day, and you will experience a profound impact in your business results!" **Kevin Knebl, co-author of The Social Media Sales Revolution**

"If you own a business or operate in a commercial environment, then Oisin's book will overcome any doubts that you have about marketing as the core business function." **Anthony Quigley, Founder & Director of the Digital Marketing Institute**

"Oisin's book is a masterpiece for any leader in any business who wants to create brand awareness, inspire brand commitment, and increase sales." **Bruce Tulgan, best-selling author of The 27 Challenges Managers Face and founder/CEO of RainmakerThinking, Inc.**

*This book is dedicated with love
to my mother,
Margaret Browne*

Contents

15 MAGIC MARKETING WORDS THAT MATTER

PREPARE, PLAN & PERFORM WITH PRECISION

USE DIGITAL MARKETING WITH CONFIDENCE

BUILD A SUPER-SOLID BUSINESS BRAND

REV UP YOUR PR ENGINE & BECOME MORE MEDIA SAVVY

MASTER YOUR MARVELLOUS MARKETING SKILLS

MEET THE MARKETING LEADERS

FOREWORD

I was intrigued when I heard that a former bin man had written a book about selling. How could that be? What was the story behind the book? I heard about Oisin Browne almost a year before I had the chance to meet him in person. That is because of the effectiveness of his marketing campaign for 'The Binman's Guide To Selling'. So it came as no surprise when I heard that he had put his fingers to the keyboard to create a guidebook of 100 ideas and inspirations about marketing.

With the continued competition for business that can come from anywhere across the globe, and with more new businesses being established everyday, there has never been a more important time to become a master at marketing if you want to grow a successful business. For the most part of my corporate career, I was fortunate to be in a business that was brand and marketing led. The organisation believed it was essential to develop marketing knowledge for all their people, no matter the function they were in. I did not have a degree in marketing and held roles spanned strategy, change management, human resources, and communications. But by the time I was ready to become an entrepreneur, I had amassed immense knowledge of marketing. This was not the case for everyone. This became clear to me as I ventured out in my own small business and meeting fellow entrepreneurs. Most business leaders and entrepreneurs never studied marketing at college, and have never held a marketing role. As Oisin references in the book, it is important to master marketing skills. You can start your own personal marketing development plan by delving into the pages of 'The Binman's Guide To Marketing'.

Let me share a little secret with you. I would skip to the back pages first. There you will find fifty inspirational interviews from marketers and entrepreneurs of large and small businesses who share their ideas and wisdom on a number of topics including what it takes to create a successful marketing campaign. That practical experience is rarely accessible and is truly invaluable. If you then return to the front section of the book, you will find one hundred ideas that Oisin shares from his experience in working with a fast growing consumer focused business, The City Bin Co. I would use this as a checklist to identify priority areas to help you benchmark how well your organisation delivers against these topics, and it will also help you understand the capabilities you need to develop either personally or within your marketing team.

There are some trends that are deep in the pages of the book that I think are worth highlighting before you start to read the book. Firstly, the idea of what Oisin calls 'marketing inward'. So many times marketing plans are focused on consumers, clients, customers, target markets, however you describe them for your organisation. A missing part is ensuring that your whole organisation understands your products and marketing plans. Many people today are talking about employees becoming 'ambassadors' for your company. That is far from a new idea and my previous organisation has valued employees as brand advocates for well over 200 years. Perhaps what is different today is that organisations are enabling their people to use social media to help promote their organisation, and social media communications on behalf of a company is no longer the domain of solely the marketing team. As I mentioned earlier, I was fortunate to have spent much of my corporate career in a marketing led company. We always sought to ensure that everyone in the organisation understood any new campaign and could be proud of them. By taking this step and engaging your people and helping them understand your campaigns. You can grow your marketing and sales team without investing another euro.

The second trend is about personalisation. We all like to be considered as being different and unique and we see an increasing trend for personalisation. Oisin suggests we personalise products with the customers' name, something that brands such as Barry's Tea, Innocent Drinks and more recently Coca Cola have done. Personalisation of marketing has also now extended into the ability to re-market with personalised messages through social advertising and online marketing. This trend will only continue to grow. Being able to master this will help you create meaningful and well targeted relevant marketing micro-campaigns.

A third trend that is worth referencing is described as 'signing up for a professional grammar course'. I personally took that a stage further by attending a creative writing skills course when I established my own business. It was probably one of the most important investments I have made in the last ten years.

Today marketers use terms such as brand journalism and content marketing. What is at the core is that we need to become master storytellers. Whether you are writing a sales page, drafting your e-zine, crafting a press release, creating the script for your online video or podcast, the words we use make a difference to the success and resonance by your target audience to your campaign.

It would be remiss of me not to tell you that there is one little thing that Oisin and I slightly differ on in the friendliest way possible! Oisin is a believer that you should always be a sales person first and a marketer second. I subscribe to the view that you should be a marketer first so that you can unlock research and insights about trends and how your products and services can be created, refined and marketed to deliver your business strategy. Unfortunately I have seen all too many businesses start up and fail because they had not fully understood how what they were trying to sell would serve the people they were trying to reach. But don't let our difference of opinion put you off delving into this book. You don't have to read the whole book and apply everything you learn at once. Find one idea that you can adopt, adapt and apply to your marketing plan then review your results and refine your plan moving forward. And remember, as Oisin says in Tip 100 – Never stop marketing!

To your marketing success!

Krishna De,
*Digital marketing, brand engagement and
social media speaker, commentator and mentor*

PREFACE

If you want to be world class at marketing, be a sales person first. If you partake in marketing activity for the feel-good factor you will go out of business very fast. Marketing has one goal: To increase sales. You make special offers to increases sales. You create brand awareness to increase sales. Your PR machine works to create an image that, in turn, increases sales. Marketing is a cog in the selling wheel. This is forgotten too often. Sometimes, the marketing experts focus on so much of the aesthetics that the return on investment can be disappointing for the client. Businesses are left with a negative impression of the benefits of marketing. Most times they do not properly understand what marketers do – the range of activities. Both the marketing and sales teams are sometimes seen as separate entities within companies when really they are one team with one goal. They need to work together to achieve success. Marketing is, in many ways, an inconspicious word for something that carries such importance when it comes to the overall effect on the bottom line of your company. Marketing is any endeavour that helps get a sale across the line. If your marketing efforts are not focused on increasing sales you can end up doing a lot of costly and irrelevant work. The more research and excellent quality marketing you do, the more likely you will make the sale with ease. It is what I call the 'seesaw effect'. The converse is equally true; vague and shallow marketing makes selling an uphill struggle.

This book is for anybody working in marketing, sales or running a business. As a sales person it will help you understand the marketing journey and where you can most seamlessly fit in. Let the marketing place the right bait in the right pond to draw in the right fish. As a sales person your job is to catch that fish! As a marketing person this book will help you focus on structuring your campaigns in a way that is measurable and successful. Use this book to dip in and out of when you are looking for ideas, inspiration, focus and structure. You will find an effective balance between the creative and the logical thinking in marketing, PR, digital media and traditional avenues. With marketing, as with sales, you need to be 'race fit'. Know you are going to win before you start the race. Once your sales mind connects to your marketing mind you will automatically think like a winner. Ask yourself of every marketing move you make: **'Will this increase my sales?'**

Marketing is the creative output of the people on the marketing team and the employees involved in getting a particular message to the right people that will entice them to buy. Marketing is the creativity within a business that separates a product from the noise of competition. It is competing to be seen, remembered and have products purchased over and over again. Marketing is a mindset that can be infused into every part of your business from employees to products to customers. A great marketer is passionate not just about the brand and the product, but also about the potential customer and their product user experience. Marketers are the ultimate sales people. They balance the freedom of creativity and brand development with a systematic framework for finding the target market. They pitch to that market and measure the success of each marketing campaign. Marketing is never-ending. From one campaign to another is how companies become great at marketing. The planning and the detail you put into each marketing campaign and your overall marketing strategy is what will build a world-class marketing machine for your business. The more comfortable a marketer can be merging new technologies with proven tactics the more likely the skill and mastery of marketing will grow. As an example of this, I am a member of a business mastermind group with social media expert, Martha Fraser. Martha says, *'Technology in the right marketing hands is like listening to a master musician.'* Martha turns 10-minute phone calls and 30-minute webinars into 10,000 dollars a pop by playing this kind of marketing music.

A strong marketing strategy is crucial to both growing and managing the perception of the brand. The marketing strategy is one of the first important steps in defining a clear path in engaging with customers. Your marketing strategy is the backbone for making your brand consistently identifiable. Commitment to preparation, planning and promotion within your marketing plan on a continuing basis is fundamental to building a better business. The world of marketing and advertising has changed completely in the last decade with the growth of online and digital tools. Marketing has become both more buyer persona focused and geo-targeted. At the same time, consumers are now well-informed on products, standards and other user experiences. They are very much in control of their purchasing and are empowered by the wealth of information online. Today, there are more businesses competing for the attention of the consumer. Today's consumer opens up their email inbox and it's full of spam and newsletters. Their post comes and it's full of junk mail. They turn on the radio and adverts run one after another. The local papers have adverts stretching from the first page to the last. To get the consumer's attention you have to understand their needs and design your marketing to speak in their language. Your approach has to be very different from everything else going on. You have to reach out on a personal level and tap into the emotional element of the buyer. For me, marketing is about listening and communicating with existing and potential customers in a clear manner. You set goals on each marketing campaign. You produce and deliver through the different platforms from digital marketing to traditional media. You measure the success of each campaign and adjust and repeat the process. In repeating this process you will sharpen your skills and refine your marketing abilities. You will see the value in following a clear plan, allowing yourself the space to make the necessary tweaks to make each campaign a success.

I started my professional life as a 'helper' on the back of a bin truck. I was collecting the bins for the commercial customers everyday. I quickly learned which businesses were busy and what days were their busiest. I could measure the success of some businesses by the amount of waste material they produced. Throughout my many years in The City Bin Co. I have gained a 360-degree perspective of business and customer relations from working on the bin trucks, in the office, on the delivery team, with the sales team, the innovation team and implemented the company's successful digital strategy and social media platforms. Today, I contribute to The City Bin Co.'s sales, marketing and innovation teams. I also work in the Middle East for averda, the largest environmental solutions provider in the MENA region.

My experience in the many different roles within The City Bin Co. and averda has given me a unique viewpoint when it comes to marketing. I believe this marketing mindset is culture driven where the focus is on customer service and sales. It comes from years of learning and practice as part of a progressive and innovative company. I have learned that we are all potential marketers with a lifetime of marketing experience – we just need to be more aware of this. Marketing has become part of everyday business for every business. It's like breathing. You have to do it, not just to survive, but also to thrive.

Oisin Browne

INTRODUCTION

This is the second book in the Binman's Guide series. Here, Oisin shares his thoughts on marketing based on his experience working in an award-winning waste collection business.

From our earliest years in business, people regularly commented how we were excellent at marketing. They would often remark that we made waste collection sexy! The strange thing was that we never had a formal marketing department or a marketing manager on our team. What we did have was two things 1) a deep insight into our own abilities and core skills, and 2) a deep insight into what our customers actually wanted from us. The secret was marrying the two.

The City Bin Co.'s marketing campaigns and brand building efforts have never been afraid of bridging the old trusted strategies and new technologies. The results of our marketing initiatives have always surpassed expectations not only with clients but also with the marketing experts, the media and bloggers. When other businesses are calling your offices asking: *'how did you do it?'* - you know you are doing something special. Well-executed marketing starts with a good idea that creates brand awareness and inspires commitment to buy from the potential customer. You don't have to outspend your competition. You can use a laser-focused strategy to level the playing field by employing innovative techniques and creativity in your marketing efforts.

The Binman's Guide to Marketing is a natural follow up to Oisin's first book on selling. Marketing and sales are two sides of the same coin. Oisin amasses his marketing wisdom from an unsexy industry across a varied customer base into a single comprehensive business book.

This book gives an exclusive insight into the dynamic world of marketing. May it inspire you and give you BIG ideas to grow your business.

Gene Browne, *CEO, The City Bin Co.*

GET THE BEST FROM THIS BOOK

The aim of this marketing book is to give people getting started in business and people already well versed in business a guide that can serve as a useful reference to all that involves marketing. It goes wide more than deep to provide a helicopter view of the marketing landscape. I haven't attempted to reinvent the wheel or go into detail on any one specific theme. The world of marketing is moving at an incredibly fast pace, especially on the digital sphere. I was very aware when writing this book that some ideas may be outdated before even going to print. As well as looking at what was in vogue, I also focus on traditional ideas that may be outdated to some, but still work in practice. They are there for you to grab and reinvent! Some ideas may seem new. Other ideas may be 'tried and tested'. Some may or may not work in some industries, while other ideas are 'on the button' in certain fields. I wanted to demonstrate the wide-ranging nature of marketing. For any business to get the most out of marketing you must dedicate time and resources to achieve effective results. Marketing results mean sales. When something clicks for you from this book that you believe would be beneficial to you or your company, set the wheels in motion by putting the idea to use. Make it yours. Bring that marketing idea to life and, more importantly, monitor and measure the progress and results.

This mix of marketing ideas and inspirations is for those with an interest in growing their business. It is for the person starting to study marketing and looking for a career in marketing. It is for the marketing and management teams of small, medium and big companies. It is a starting point; a source of ideas to apply to your marketing endeavours. All marketing starts with an idea. Let this book be your guide to finding those great ideas that will ultimately turn into sales. Allow yourself to be creative and innovative. These chapters are designed to be short and sweet. They are easy to flick through. There is not so much information that you will go astray, yet there are enough ideas and inspirations to keep you hooked.

As with the first book, **The Binman's Guide to Selling**, this book is deliberately written in a way that allows you to randomly open it at any point and start reading at any particular page you choose. It is written to encourage creative thinking that can be applied to your marketing activity. No matter what stage you are at in your marketing career, it is always helpful to have somewhere to draw additional creativity from. This is your book, so be sure to write on it, add to it and highlight the parts that you find interesting and useful. Enjoy the read and give yourself a good dose of idea generating inspiration!

15 MAGIC MARKETING WORDS THAT MATTER

Words are powerful. They encourage the sale. They trigger images. They can make a suggestion. The can guide you to act. They can motivate people to buy. They can be the tipping point in making a sale. Business is founded on the concept of marketing and selling a product or service to make a profit. When it comes to writing your marketing materials, the words that you use must turn cold calls to warm leads with the intention to get them to make a purchase. Choosing the right words for your marketing material will impact your bottom line. Using magic marketing words that matter can lead to magic numbers in your sales funnel. There is an art to writing great marketing messages that hook the masses. Writing the right marketing message takes time and skill. You have to creatively compose a communication where you have to say a lot with limited wording. You have to get inside the mind of the potential customer. The right words can turn great ideas into sales. It's worth developing your marketing vocabulary. Start by looking at what works for others. When you see a message that resonates with the public or that is part of a successful marketing campaign investigate the motive. Learn what words to avoid. Look at images that accompany the words. Research and learn who gets it wrong and why it didn't work. You can say the wrong thing with the right words and you can say the right thing with the wrong words. This can be expensive in terms of time, energy and loss of sales. Look for words that sit well with your culture. Think about the language used in the day-to-day running of your company both internally and externally. When creating copy, find the right words to use. What is your natural tone? Different marketing words work well in different situations and on different material. You have to define the right language for your audience. You will find your potential target market by researching and testing different marketing words with focus test groups. Their response will tell you the words that work and those that do not work. Think about how language affects emotions and encourages potential clients to take action. For your potential customer to tune in to your message you have to dial in and say the right thing in the right language. Listen to your existing customers to find suitable words that attract your potential customers. The 15 words on the following pages are strong foundation words that will give you a starting point to build your marketing message. Why have you seen these familiar words before? The answer is easy: because they work!

1. FREE

How it Works

The best things in life are not **free**! The word **free** is one of the most overused words in marketing and it works. It grabs people's attention; it's engaging. It is also one of the most misleading words in marketing as nothing is really free. There is a cost to everything, be it time or money. Somebody, somewhere pays. Use the word free to encourage customers to buy products at full price. Free is a powerful incentive that can increase your orders - when used correctly.

What to Say

I'm not a fan of *'buy one, get one free'* or *'buy two for the price of one.'* While the word free attracts new customers, that fact is you have just created a new price. This will be making less money per product than before. Be careful not to create a new lower price in your customer's mind. When this happens it can be a race to the bottom with competitors reacting by imitating your offer. The customer wins, not because they value your product, but because they are looking for the cheap deals. Once your offer changes or the price increases, how will you keep that customer from trying a different brand when they are only tuned into the dollar signs?

I am not saying don't use the word free. In fact, I encourage it once you eliminate the risk of losing the product's inherent value.

Nordstrom, the American fashion retailer, have a free shipping, free returns policy. On their website they tell their customers:

*'We'll **ship** almost anything on our site to anywhere in the U.S. for **free**. If you don't love it, return it for **free**, too!'*

Use Free in a powerful way that shows how valuable your product is by offering a free sample, free shipping, free upgrade, free download, free demo, set yourself free or first month is free when you purchase a year's worth of product. Free is a powerful incentive that can increase your orders when used correctly.

How you use it and where you use it is important. Be aware that word free in E- mails and on advertisement brochures can set the spam and junk mail alarm bells going.

2. SAVE

How it Works

The mighty marketing word **save** is great for showing the money and time that one saves when committing to buy a product. Everybody wants to save money. Using **save** in your marketing copy communicates the fact that you are not only saving, but you are gaining. You save by purchasing an offer or product at a certain price and you are gaining by having the product and benefits of the product once you make the purchase.

What to Say

Saving is the opposite of spending, yet we use it in marketing to ask people to spend! The word save plays on the necessity of potential customers who wish to reduce their costs. Potential buyers want to know that they will save time, money or themselves!

"Save money and live better', 'Smile and save. You'll be 10% better off at Asda' and *'Save money and time. Shop your way'* is the language used by the marketing proffesionals at the retail giant ASDA

'When you buy our starter pack and deluxe pack together, you will **save** *yourself 10% on your purchase. That is money in your pocket!'*

*'***Save*** yourself from burnout by signing up to our weekly yoga sessions for busy business people.'*

'You will **save** *time, energy and effort when you apply the Binman's Guide system to your business.'*

When people are buying a product, they are more interested in getting what they perceive as a great deal than paying a rock bottom price. The word **save** frames this very well. Nobody wants to be seen as cheap, however, if they saved money by getting a genuine bargain, that's something to talk about and share with their family, friends and colleagues.

3. BUY NOW

How it Works

Buy now, act now, switch and save today, are all **calls to actions**. They look for an action or desired outcome. The purpose of a call to action is to persuade potential customers to respond immediately. *Simply call us today, sign up* and *register today* are more examples of common calls to actions.

The call to action is intended to improve the market's response rate to your marketing message. If you don't ask somebody to do something, they may forget or do nothing, or simply say *'that's interesting'* and move on. As in sales, it's the same in marketing: **If you don't ask you don't get!**

What to Say

Ask the potential buyer to do something. When you use a call to action you trigger an immediate response. To have success when using a clear call to action include a limited-time offer or a deadline.

*'**Switch today** and join the thousands that have already experienced the true value and security of using our products.'*

'Apply best practices to your business with our 12 week course
*- How to apply the Binman's Guide to your business. **Subscribe today**.'*

*'**Act now** and we'll get you free access to our online executive members area for the next 2 months.'*

A great marketing call to action will prompt a response right away. When you give people an option to wait and think about it, the chances are they won't take the offer. Never look for a commitment or a contract with this particular approach. A call to action is really reaching out to the potential client and saying: *'Take a closer look. We think you will like it. If you do we have a special once off offer for you today; no obligation.'*

If people follow through, make sure there is some place for them to go or some action that they can take such as a phone number or *'click here'* sign up button. Make the next action after they accept your call to action as easy as pie for the prospective customer or client.

4. FINAL

How it Works

There is nothing like the fear of loss when it comes to marketing and sales. The word **final** in the copy of a marketing campaign certainly creates that. When you communicate to potential customers that a special offer has a deadline it creates a sense of urgency.

What to Say

Give your potential customers a specific timeframe on all offers.

'***Final*** *chance to clean up at the spring sale. Offer ends this Friday!*'

'***Final*** *days to sign up to the grow your business marketing course.*'

Marketing campaign responses tend to peak coming up to the **final days** of any offer. This is when you need to change the message and add the sense of necessity. Issue a press release or newsletter stating how successful your campaign, promotion, sale, or product launch went. Alert your audience to the fact that this date is the final day.

Build a real sense of '***If you are not in, you can't win.***'

The word final is a connection word that creates emotional links from one season, event or important day to another, for example:

'*Now that the **final** days of summer are over, we are preparing for the busy back to school shopping season.*'

'*Time to get ready for a good spring-cleaning as the **final** days of winter come to an end. Put a little sun into your life and order a skip this weekend. Order now and you will be in with a chance to win a weekend away.*'

Businesses who do not have enough stock to cover potential demand in the final days of the sale can risk losing sales. Have a plan B if stock runs out.

5. GUARANTEE

How it Works

Anybody that buys a product takes a risk. There is always a chance of disliking the product for one reason or another. Placing a **guarantee** on the purchase reduces the likelihood of loss. If they don't want or like the purchase or the before purchase perception doesn't meet the after purchase expectation, they simply return it. Giving a good 'guarantee' on the purchase is more attractive than a guarantee on the product itself. You take the risk out of the buying for the potential customer and that automatically makes the offering more attractive. And that's without dropping the price! Do your marketing successfully and attract the right potential customers: people who use what you sell. You are making a small commitment to these potential buyers that your product is so good and they will be so satisfied with their purchase that returning it will not be on the radar. If you are getting a lot of returns you need to look at two things. Firstly, look at the quality of your product. Secondly, start profiling your target market.

What to Say

Keep it simple and to the point. If more detail is needed you can have it in your terms and conditions.

Stewart-MacDonald, a guitar supply store operating out of Athens, Ohio tell their customers: *'Our guarantee since 1968:100% satisfaction in every way. If any item fails to meet your expectations, please return it, unaltered, for a refund or exchange.'*

CogniView, a leading provider of data conversion software give their customers the following guarantee: *'100% refund for 30 days – no questions asked! To prove our confidence in the products we provide and their value to you, we are offering a 30-day, money-back **guarantee**'*

If you have a money back guarantee, or a service guarantee, make sure it's up front on your marketing copy. It relaxes the potential customer by taking the risk out of any transaction for the potential customer.

A guarantee isn't just for money back policies. You can guarantee the lifespan of a product, the service that you deliver or the expected results. Map out your customer's touch points with your product and see what you can guarantee.

6. NEW

How it Works

Everybody likes to have something **new**. New can imply that your product is progressive and leading the way in your industry. New is exciting and shiny. New can be a solution to a potential customer's objection; new fixes the problem. New develops more benefits. New improves the features. Customers and potential clients can get bored of stagnant offers and repeated marketing messages. The word new helps to get them all excited again. New can indicate innovation and a brand's attempt to improve a product, price, design or user experience.

What to Say

Customers associate the word new with an improved version of what they already love. Apple iPhones are famous for their new improved design with each new model. This creates a desire amongst their existing clients who go out and buy the latest model, yet there was technically nothing wrong or inadequate with the phone they had. To imply something is new tells your audience that it is improved, exciting, and different.

Use new to suggest to your potential clients that it is time to give their existing habits, products or suppliers the boot!

*'A **new** year, a **new** you; Out with the old and in with the **new**. Let our products transform you today.'*

You can use new to tell your customers that you have listened to them and taken onboard their suggestions:

*'We have taken your feedback on board. We redesigned what you already loved and created a **new** version. Upgrade today and experience the difference.'*

7. DISCOVER

How it Works

Every child loves to **discover** something new. They are natural born explorers. In asking somebody to discover, you are tapping into the childhood memories on an emotional level. You are giving them permission to take a closer look. Guiding your potential customer to discover for themselves the pleasures of using your product is to say: Don't ask me; try it for yourself. You are asking them to go on a journey. You are encouraging them to take a chance. When you use discover you are suggesting that there is something new that the potential client may be interested in. It's the same as saying: *'Hey, look at this.'* The important thing is to have something worth seeing when they come calling. If your product is the same old story, you risk losing them on the first step.

What to Say

Discover is a guarantee of something interesting to bring the potential customer a little closer. Like the child discovering things for the first time, there needs to be a sense of anticipation, enthusiasm and exploration. When you arouse those warm childhood emotions you have the attention and potential for an easier sale.

The description on the back of my first book read:

*'**Discover** the secrets of selling with this collection of easy to read powerful words, strategies, tips, scripts, interviews and inspirations.'*

Spain's Bank of Santander ran an advert with the capture: *'**Discover** the freedom of a Santander mortgage.'*

Thomson Holidays tagged their brand on their TV advert with *'**Discover** your Smile!'*

Use it to build trust with your customers by bringing them on the product journey. John West does this by inviting its customers to trace the origins of the fish with their *'**Discover** the story behind your can.'* Section on their website.

8. EASY

How it Works

Everything is about being **easy**! It has to be easy to buy, easy to access, easy to assemble, easy to use, easy to fix and easy to communicate with the customer support team. An easy to deal with business and product come in top of the agenda when it comes to potential customers buying products. Easy means that the actions taken to buy or engage with you, your business and your products are quick and instant. Easy means making it simple for customers to purchase the product, and when they do get it that it will be easy to use. Nobody wants to be left waiting or to read manuals about the product. You are competing in a commercial world where so much is about instant access. People are looking for the seamless user experience.

What to Say

Focus on the customer touch points for your product and business to see where your product or services are easy. Look at where you can improve the customer's journey. Once you find them, highlight them. Sometimes, we spend too much time boosting the benefits of the product without mentioning the words that will get the sale over the line: *easy, easier and easiest.* These words can solve a whole host of problems. Look at what is easy about using your product and promote it.

'It's as **easy** *as 1,2,3.'*

'Using our products is so **easy** *you would not even know you are wearing them.'*

'We will make the changeover so seamless that the only change you will notice is how **easy** *everything has become.'*

'Our customers say the best thing about our service is that it is so **easy** *to contact us.'*

9. OFFER

How it Works

To say that you are offering something at a discount or offering something new is to give a shout out to your audience and say *'Hey, listen here a moment!'* Be sure you have a great **offer** or you will lose their attention very fast. The word offer can have different meanings depending on the message you are communicating.

What to Say

To offer something fantastic or to introduce a new offer is one angle:

*'Introducing the brand new **offer** from The Browne Brothers this Friday night. We invite you to this once-off launch with special guests and give you a chance to sample our new range of products.'*

Your potential customers are on the lookout for offers. They are looking for new exciting deals. The word offer often implies a sale or a bargain, so it's important that if you bring a new offer to the table that you clearly state that it's an introductory offer.

*'For the month of July only you can buy this special introductory **offer**.'*

To place your existing products on sale is another way to use the word.

*'Special **offer**: 20% off - today only.'*

Always state that it's a limited offer available only during a specified time frame. As with all marketing words, the word offer may have one meaning for you and a different meaning for your potential customer. Be clear on the meaning for the customer, as their understanding and interpretation is paramount.

10. LIMITED

How it Works

To set a limit and market a limit around your product helps you to create a sense of urgency about buying your product. The word **limited** requests immediate action. One might say that being limited is a negative thing, but not if you are referring to a product or an offer. A limited edition product or an offer for a limited time can double your revenue. This tells the potential customer that it is now or never. Using the word limited forces an instantaneous response from those who are interested in your restricted or limited edition offer.

What to Say

Limited gives a strong sense of exclusivity in your potential customer's mind. It adds value to your product because it is limited in some way; a rare edition or a short timeframe.

Place a time limit on your campaign and offer your top line products at the price point that maybe in reach of new potential customers:

*'For a **limited** time only, you will receive all our high value range at a base value price. We want you to experience what 80 percent of our customers are enjoying today.'*

Or

*'This high value offer is **limited** to 10 orders only.'*

*'Don't miss out on an opportunity to own a special **limited** edition of our product - available today only.'*

When launching a campaign invite potential customers to a limited trial of your product. This way you find out who are your product ambassadors.

*'Come to our **limited** trial pre-launch so you can be the first to sampleour new product.!'*

11. SECRET

How it Works

The word **secret** promotes mystery and uniqueness in the mind of the potential customer. You are letting them know that you will give them access to precious knowledge that will be of benefit to them. You are saying that your offer is an exclusive product especially for selected individuals.

What to Say

In November 2015, I was walking along *The High Line*, a popular park walk 30 feet above street level on an old rail line in New York. From there, I saw a big yellow billboard from parkfast.com that overlooked their parking lot. It said: *'So you can't parallel park. It will be our little **secret**.'*

After the walk I remember entering the metro station to return to central park where I came across an advert for Sephora, a beauty retail giant. The advert simply stated: *'We don't keep beauty **secrets**.'* Followed by the store locations.

Use secret to convey that you have the solution. It also gives value to the solution providng nobody else knows the secret!

*'We have the key to your fitness success. We will reveal the **secret** directly to you when you sign up to our offer.'*

*'Learn the top **secrets** of a clean home when you try our new state of the art home air freshener.'*

*'Europe's best kept **secret** is here: Limited edition. Only 1000 units made. When they are gone, they're gone. Don't be left behind!'*

There is, of course, a contradiction in saying that you have a secret, yet you want everybody to know about it and talk about. Secrets create suspense and a longing to know more.

*'**Secrets** are **secrets** for a reason, but the good **secrets** are worth spreading: pick up our product today and find out why?'*

12. YOU

How it Works

You is the magic word of marketing and can turn the loud communications into soft-spoken personal messages. It's the key that opens the door to the emotional buyer. Although your marketing goes out to the masses, you want it to speak to the individual. To do this, use **you**. The conversation is on display publicly, but you want the message received privately. You need the passing eyes to feel like you are speaking to them in a direct and personal way. The word you give this impression and makes that marketing conversation happen. It gives direction and suggestions, which encourage action from the potential customers.

What to Say

People are normally focused on themselves and their own issues. This is simply human nature. Tune into that fact. Make your marketing message about them.

'**You** are the reason.'

'When **you** sign up to our online program **you** will receive 2 months free giving **you** the insight into the best diet plans. **You** can do it. The product just gives **you** the tools to succeed.'

'Made especially for **you**, because **you** are one of a kind.'

You are addressing the individual; the single person. When you do that and do it correctly you can tap into the emotional energy of your potential client.

13. VALUE

How it Works

Some might say run-of-the-mill marketing words are best avoided. They can be too common which is true, but they work. They are the foundation of creating great copy. Your message needs strong words that help you convey the **value** of what you are selling. The word value can help you ground your message. Tap into buyer emotions by adding value to what they care about the most. Give value to your product and brand by making it stand out for being different. Do this through story telling. Let the most appropriate words push through to the surface. Get creative with your storytelling. Tell the story with a picture. Tell the same story with words. Say it in a sentence. Tell it in three words. Tell it in one word. If you can't find the words, go back to the one basic word that sells: VALUE. Oscar Wilde said, *'Nowadays people know the **price** of everything and the **value** of nothing.'* It's your job to convey the value.

What to Say

The customer wants value and you must want to give value in return. The best way to do this is to spell it out.

*'The **value** you will receive from using our products is x,y, and z.'*

*'Let us add **value** to your day by doing x,y,and z.'*

*'If you don't get **value** after one day on this course, we will return your fee. No questions asked. Sign up today.'*

*'True **value** is what happens when you invest in yourself. Invest in yourself today and experience the difference.'*

14. LOVE

How it Works

Love isn't just reserved for Valentine's Day. You want your customers to be in love with your products and your brand. You must love your customers. You must love your own products. You must love service. If you tick all those boxes, the best thing you can show your potential clients is the love you have for your existing customers and the love they have for your products. Don't look for another word to express this special adoration. Use the word love itself. It's an honest and powerful emotional motivator.

What to Say

To know that somebody likes a product, needs a product, wants a product is good; but to love a product, that's commitment with belief, trust and experience. Express love. Some of the biggest brands in the world do it repeatedly:

Delta Airlines use *'You will love the way we fly.'* And *'We **love** to fly and it shows.'* in their marketing message.

A personal favourite of mine is Calvin Klein whose tagline reads: *'Between **love** and madness lies obsession.'*

When love is expressed, the association is more likely to be immediate and effective. It seeks to convince the potential customer that they will be as fully satisfied as existing customers are. Declare your love by saying things such as:

*'We are so head over heels in **love** with you because you wear our shoes!'*

*'Give yourself a little **love** by visiting any of our stores today.'*

*'We believe for a flower to grow you have to feed it with **love**. Call in and let us share some of that **love**!'*

*'We **love** service'* was the message of one of The City Bin Co.'s marketing campaigns. This reinforced a message that customer service is a priority and the standards are high.

15. RESULTS

How it Works

For you, results revolve around selling a product or service. For your customer, results are based on their user experience meeting their precieved expections. When it comes to writing your marketing material the word **results** will help you turn your potential prospects into new customers. Results means proof of success. Businesses demand results. Sales people aim for targeted and forecasted results. Customers expect results. If your customers aren't getting results with your product you are certainly not receiving the results you desire. If you have 100 percent faith in your product and have proof of results from your existing customers, let everyone else know about these results. You sell what you sell because you are selling solutions and you want results. Customers buy from you because they are filling a need and they want results. If your customers don't get results, you are going to find business hard. If you focus on getting results for your customers first, your result will automatically follow. If you demonstrate to your audience of potential buyers that they can get the desired satisfaction from using your products they will come back again. They will become part of your sales team. They will be your product ambassadors.

What to Say

There are many different results for you to focus on from real guaranteed results to powerful, new and instant results. You have economical, financial, emotional and premium results. The list goes on. When you can stand behind what you sell you can say with great conviction:

*'Real **results** guaranteed every time.'*

Make a promise to your future clients that will entice them to buy:

*'Commit to our service and we will commit to your **results**.'*

*'Our only purpose is to deliver you successful **results** with the products that we have built. We have built these products by listening to our existing customers.'*

*'Stick with us. The **results** speak for themselves.'*

PREPARE, PLAN & PERFORM
WITH PRECISION

A good recipe only works if you get the ingredients right. It's no different when it comes to the commitment you put into your marketing mix. When you fail to prepare you must prepare to fail. It's the difference between being proactive in determining the outcome as opposed to being reactive to spontaneous situations. You would not sit an exam without learning and studying for it beforehand. A healthy objective would be to aim for the high numbers and pass with flying colours. You would not do your driving test without putting in the practice. The goal is to pass the test with confidence. To prepare, plan and perform is to have permission to succeed. By mapping out your route to success you can identify your potential bottleneck points and deal with them well in advance. You can design your campaigns to be responsive to the rapidly changing environment of your potential client. In researching your potential customers, competitors and the market, you can tailor your offering with a unique strategic direction that helps you reach your targets. You can measure business outcomes and see opportunities that would not be visible if you did not do your homework. You can make informed decisions on each step of your campaign when you put in the groundwork. You can evaluate the risks. You can make better choices based on facts instead of guesswork. You can decide to go on or to go back to the drawing board. When you know your forecasted expenditure and your customer acquisition cost, you can plan your success route with precision. There is a certain confidence and sense of security when you know where you are going, how you are going to get there, what it will cost and all possible distractions that may befall your journey. In fact, you will more than likely get there faster and have more fun on the way.

Take time to prepare so that you can understand your competitors, your market, and most importantly, your existing and potential customers. Think about outside factors such as political and environmental elements that could affect your offering. Create a step-by-step approach that enables you to gauge progress and make clear decisions. Put energy into product development to make sure you are meeting the needs of your customers in terms of product, quality and price. Design your marketing plans with short term and long term goals that can be measured. Revisit, review and replan your marketing regularly. Read and measure it in real time. Great preparation and planning will result in clarity. Clarity gives focus. Focus leads to success.

16. THE 10 STAGES OF MARKETING (THAT SELL)

How it Works

When you select your target market wisely and refine it, you will be able to satisfy the right potential customers all of the time. The marketing landscape has many roads that you can take from beginning to end when following a plan to launch a campaign. Taking a step-by-step approach will allow you to advance your marketing in a focused way and turn your ideas into invoices.

What to Do

1. **Define your audience.** Running a marketing campaign or designing a plan without defining your audience can cause you to lose both your time and money. To achieve a good return on investment, you must send the right message to the right market using the right media. Start by creating a complete profile description of your ideal customer; the person that will pay you for your product. Go into detail on their buying habits. Identify why they will buy your product. To find this information, dig deep into your current pool of customers by asking questions.

2. **Craft a great offer.** This is the message that tells your potential customers what you are offering them for their hard-earned cash and why it's a perfect and obvious fit. Once you know your target audience, design your offering for them. Speak their language. Use their tone. Tap into their interests. Grab their attention. Focus on your headline. Make it your hook. Tell your story. Explain the benefits. Tell them the problems that your product solves. Remove any risk by providing a guarantee or a brand promise. Have a strong call to action.

3. **Create your target goal.** Set a goal that you know you can actually achieve. Study and understand your target market. Have a clear end result. Have your main goals and supporting goals. State the different elements of the campaign and your expected daily sales target from each marketing action. Think **BIG** when setting your goal, but stay realistic.

4. **Decide your budget**. Knowing the limit on your spend is not an invitation to throw it away. You have to be cost effective. Work within your own means. Look at the digital marketing tools that allow you to reach your target audience with laser focus such as your website and social platforms like LinkedIn, Facebook, and Twitter. These can all be micro-measured giving you great bang for your buck. Have a base budget for your design, artwork and printing. Hold back a reserve fund in case you have to pull the plug and start again on any aspect of your plan. Calculate your return on investment before you spend a cent. This will give you a high-tide mark and avoid getting stuck in the mud.

5. **Develop a campaign** Start with the end in mind. Map out your marketing plan on a timeline Show the day-by-day actions so you can storyboard how everything will happen from start to finish. Get a good core team of 4 to 5 people around you. They can give your development a 360-degree view of the marketing opportunity that you need to form. Create a collaborative mix that will fill in any lack of expertise by going outside your company employees. Where possible invite customers, non-customers, entrepreneurs and marketing specialists to join you for your campaign.

6. **Write a clear marketing message.** Your potential new customers don't care about your product or solution. They only care about their problems or situation. Address their problems with crystal clear communication. Give them the expectation that their problem can be solved easily for a fee. Keep your message short and simple. Say it with as few words as possible. Say it with a picture. Have a clear call to action. Ask for the business.

7. **Hire a professional to design the copy and graphics**. Good copy and graphic design can generate powerful communication with your target market. If you have no experience in this area, engage a professional to take your visuals to success. They will help you design an imaginative vision and message that appeals to your audience. Having a talented designer as part of your creative team will greatly help in the management of your marketing campaign.

8. **Produce and deliver the piece.** The pressure is on once you set your campaign launch date. Know the lead-time needed for the creation of content and the printing or recording. When engaging with media outlets, call well in advance to find out deadlines and lead times needed for promotional material.

9. **Measure your marketing success.** To master marketing you must measure it. Measure your marketing against the sales produced in the marketing time frame. Everything can be measured from footfall to social media, from click-throughs to transactions. Pick your top 5 metrics with the top being sales. Set targets on each metric. If you are not reaching your targets, tweak the campaign message or offering. If you are reaching you targets, well you know what they say, 'If it's not broken, don't try to fix it!'

10. **Repeat the process.** Don't become guilty of running one campaign and hanging up the boots until the next time. When you are finished your marketing campaign, you need to review your results with a view of keeping the tap dripping. As soon as you have studied and learned the lesson, start the process again. The budget may not be in it but there is so much that can be created without a big cost. Think about email marketing with discount offers, and press releases that tell your success story. Push the go button on the marketing machine continuously to master your marketing ability and ultimately to sell more.

Tips and Take Homes

Always be honest in your message. Don't make promises you can't keep. Deliver your messages in a meaningful and memorable manner. Be flexible enough to allow change at any point of the campaign that will improve your results and lead to better sales.

Digital Nugget

No matter what you sell, be sure to have an online shop, a 'join us' page, a request a 'call back' button or a sign up form that will enable a potential customer to make a purchase outside your normal working hours.

17. THE 3 E'S OF A SUCCESSFUL MARKETING PLAN

How it Works

There are numerous templates and strands to follow when planning a successful marketing plan. The core of all great strategies contain the following 3 E's:

1. Examination
2. Execution
3. Evaluation

Your marketing plan is a work in progress that will become a masterpiece with the right marketing strategy. Commitment to preparation, planning and promotion of your plan on a continuous basis is fundamental to building a better business. Time in the examination period will pay off in the execution stage and give you the tools to be better prepared for the evaluation phase.

What to Do

Examination is all about market research, market analysis, planning and preparation. Don't do it all on your own. Get a team together. If your company is big enough, invite people from different departments with different skills and talents. If your team is too small to pull on the company's resources, recruit your team externally. Invite a marketing professional; a customer, a business school professor and other business colleagues whom you believe will contribute and enhance your project. Ask them for one hour a week of their professional input in exchange for being part of something exciting, a sample pack of your product or an invite to lunch. People love to help people and love to be part of something that is exciting and new.

Start by defining your objectives. What is the realistic end-goal? What do you want to achieve? Design a strategy timeline that clearly sets out the steps needed to reach your end-goal. Apply basic old school academic marketing exercises such as a SWOT analysis, the 4 P's, the 5 C's and the 6 M's. I'll explain these below.

A **SWOT** analysis is commonly used to identify opposition and opportunities for a new business plan or a marketing campaign. **SWOT** is an acronym for:

1. Strengths
2. Weaknesses
3. Opportunities
4. Threats

Pinpointing these will allow you to identify all positive and negative elements that may affect any new proposed actions.

Break down the elements of your offering and define your target market by applying the 4 P's. These four strategic points contain the basic essentials of marketing which will help you define your offering. They will help you focus your energies to get the best probability of achievement within your target market. **The 4 P's** are:

1. Product
2. Place
3. Price
4. Promotion

Think about your product in terms of features, brand, and quality. Choose the places where your product will be distributed offline and online and to whom it will be made available. Calculate the price and create a price structure around your offering. Gauge the customer acquisition cost to you and the perceived value cost to your customer. Consider what promotional channels you will use such as advertising, public relations, direct marketing, social media and promotional events.

The 5 C's gives you a valuable guide to study the current state of the industry and marketplace. It allows you to make a good assessment of the existing market conditions further enabling you to track calculated decisions in driving your business.

The 5 C's are:

1. **Customers**: When you look at *customers* focus on the demographics, the core needs of the customer, the persona profile, their budget, where and when they buy, the market size and its potential to grow.

2. **Company**: Look at your *company* and its competencies. Look at your products and offerings. Where are you in the market and where do you wish to be? Is your business aligned with the market requirements? Where is the market going? And where are you going? Are you in line to achieve your goals?

3. **Competitors:** Study your *competitors*. Why are they successful? Where are they successful and why are you different? Look at them online. What does the market think about your competition? What are your competitor's strengths and weaknesses?

4. **Collaborators:** Look at the *collaborators* within your business. Identify the capabilities and performance needed to make your business a success. Look at product suppliers, distributors, partners and agencies. Learn to identify who you need to make your business work. What's the relationship between their performance and the efficiency of your business? Have you had any issues with subcontractors or suppliers? How likely are they to recur?

5. **Climate:** Establish the *climate* aspects in which your business operates. Some of the key factors include the political, economic, technological, cultural, regulatory and social conditions. What do you know that's true about the climate in which your business operates and what do you not know?

Another tool to apply to your plan is the 6 M's of marketing. **The 6 M's are:**

1. **Market:** Who is the audience that you will be addressing?
2. **Mission**: What are the goals of your marketing efforts?
3. **Message**: What is the one message to be communicated?
4. **Media**: What platforms will you use?
5. **Money**: What is your budget and how will it be spent?
6. **Measurement:** How will you measure the campaign during and after?

These tools will best position you to design your campaign. You will be better positioned to have a more creative input when delivering the right message. You will build awareness with the right audience. You will push your call to action at the right time. Take time to plan. Don't be tempted to rush. Complete the groundwork first.

Execution is the application and amendment of the plan in real time throughout the campaign. This phase is always going to be a work in progress. The plan will evolve as real-time events unfold. When you have your strategy worked out and you know exactly how you're going to tell your story in order to make yourself and your business visible, you need to become comfortable with the idea that you may have to change and adapt. Be prepared to change if the market doesn't believe you, if you are selling too little or if you are selling too much. Create the short-term objectives and daily to-do lists that will help you move your product. Set a start date and a completion date for your campaign. Draw up a timeline with key promotion dates, expected actions and anticipated targets. Assign tasks to the appropriate members of your team and review daily. They need to be long term and goal oriented. Like an artist painting a picture, paint and repaint. Sometimes you will need to go back to the blank canvas in order to arrive at a masterpiece. It may take months or even years to get the masterpiece perfect. Never stop because it's not working. Keep working with it until it works. This is execution.

Evaluation concerns the testing of the product and measuring key metrics against forecast objectives. This attention to detail allows for change that keeps the plan moving forward to a clearly defined goal. For your business to be noticed, you need to work and rework your strategy. You must revisit and rewrite the plan regularly. You need to get excited about it. You must execute it. When you have your strategy worked out and you know exactly how you're going to tell your story in order to make yourself and your business visible, you need to become comfortable with the idea that you may have to change and adapt it. Business and marketing strategies should not be seen as something you do for a week or two and hope for the best. For your business to be noticed you need to work and rework your strategy continuously. You need to continually advertise your wares. Commitment to preparation, planning and promotion of your company on continuous basis is fundamental to building a better business. If you are not marketing you have nothing to evaluate. Evaluation encourages high performance through routine spot-checks and targets focused benchmarking.

Tips and Take Homes

Turn your marketing plan into a live case study by blogging about every step, success and failure along the way. This is a great way to connect with businesses that wish to create a marketing plan like yours. You don't have to expose trade secrets. Share the human aspect of the campaign; what's happening behind the scenes and what you are learning.

If you record a TV commercial, you can make a two-minute fly on the wall behind-the-scenes documentary video. You can blog about the team behind the creative input. This also creates a feeling of transparency and trust with your customer.

Digital Nugget

You need to be seen and heard. You need to review your approach frequently. Today's businesses are lucky to have huge no cost resources online such as YouTube, Facebook and Twitter. Use them. These new outlets of distribution for your business message can be the tipping point you need for complementing your story or advert campaign in the tradition medias. They allow your minor efforts to become momentous and trigger a more significant difference in your overall marketing.

18. CALULATE YOUR CUSTOMER ACQUISITION COST

How it Works

How much does it cost you to obtain one new customer? If you knew your cost per action or the return on your marketing spend before you started, it would possibly shape the strategy of all your future marketing activities. The total cost connected to convincing a customer to purchase your product is your customer acquisition cost (CAC). When you know your CAC, you can evaluate the quantity of new customers needed to reimburse the delivery of your marketing efforts. You can estimate the number of new customers needed to make X amount of margin. A lot of businesses simply don't bother to work this out. Some business people work it out *after* their marketing campaign is long over. The right time to calculate your CAC is *before* you start any marketing activity.

What to Do

Your CAC is the cost required for your research, time, all offline and online marketing expenditure, advertising, people and the products. The best way to estimate your CAC is your total marketing campaigns spend divided by the number of new customers within a particular timeframe. The advantage of analysing the numbers on a day-to-day metric as it happens is that it will allow you to make better decisions. When you have this information on tap, you can adjust your spend accordingly and fine-tune your marketing strategy if the numbers aren't stacking up. Create a formula that suits you and your type of business.

Tips and Take Homes

Strictly speaking, there is no right answer to the CAC question as marketing campaigns can have many hidden costs and different pricing models. Markets can be unpredictable.

Digital Nugget

Start a pre-marketing campaign separately on one or two online platforms where you can test and tweak your offering to give you the best results before going into a full scale launch. This can help you forecast more accurate results later in your marketing campaign.

19. CREATE MISSION, VISION AND PURPOSE STATEMENTS

How it Works

Your brand **Mission**, **Vision** and **Purpose** gives focus and clarity to what you do, why you do it and where you are going. Apart from the creation of your product or service, these are 3 very important declarations that you will use to service the right clients. They will help you market your products with the right language. They will inspire you and your team to reach your goals and, just as importantly, inspire others who want to do business with you. These statements are fundamental in guiding you, your team, your existing clients and potential customers towards understanding what you do and why.

What to Do

Keep your mission, value and purpose statements short, clear and concise. When creating your statements, they should answer certain questions, which define your purpose for being in business. It should outline your goals and explain your core motive for existing. Think about the needs you are addressing in your industry and for your clients. Why do you need to address these needs? And, in doing so, what problems do you solve for your clients? Make them real and achievable. An example of mission, value and purpose statements that are kept to the point and clear is that of The City Bin Co.

- *Our **Mission** is to be the global service leader in our industry.*

- *Our **Vision** is to raise standards worldwide by taking our service model to the international stage.*

- *Our **Purpose** is to provide excellent customer service experiences.*

Tips and Take Homes

Avoid waffle and business buzzwords. Keep it simple enough for all to understand without an explanation. A mission statement is often what sets one company apart from the competition. Test your statements by placing it beside your competitors'. It should stand out and put you in a unique and desired position.

Digital Nugget

Use your statements to speak to customers online. These clear statements give you a language to use when communicating in pictures and words. Place them on your homepage so all can see exactly who you are, what you believe and where you are going.

20. CUT YOUR METRICS TO MEASURE

How it Works

We have all heard the saying: *'What gets measured gets done.'* It's no different in marketing. Measure everything everywhere. Pick the top 5 to 10 key performance indicators (KPI's) relevant to your goals. If you have an online platform achieving zero to any other number, measure it. When you measure movement over a length of time you can pinpoint patterns that can accurately tell you where you are strong and where you need to change. If you know how many visitors come to your website and how many are making purchases, when they are making purchases and where they are sourced, you can tweak your campaigns to speak and sell to a particular audience.

What to Do

Link your marketing metrics to the bottom line to give your marketing activity a cost-effectiveness focus. Consider all measurable factors when creating your marketing KPI's. You can divide your metrics into 2 divisions:

1. Qualitative metric (The experience)
2. Quantitative metric (The numbers)

The **qualitative metric** consists of brand awareness, customer satisfaction, goodwill and likeability. The numbers may not directly link to a sale but without it the sale may not happen. Also, within the digital field you have the qualitative measurement of engagement from reach to followers and subscribers. If you have a website you need to measure visits against page click through rate, purchases and drop off rates. If you are running campaigns measure your cost per click, bounce rate and your conversion rate.

The **quantitative metric** includes statistics such as customer acquisition, expenses, sales, estimated margins, and profit and loss. Included in the quantitative metric is your digital metrics of website click throughs to direct sales. You may argue you don't need this because you are not really online. I would say that statement is an indicator of how much you need to focus on the digital arena.

Tips and Take Homes

When you have your marketing KPI's, follow each KPI with a weekly action plan. The data is live and you need to react in real time to the data to have maximum impact. Remember, you can measure everything but that doesn't mean you need to look at everything. Keep the metrics meaningful and relevent.

Digital Nugget

There are plenty of easy-to-use online lead conversation and engagement tools such as *Salesforce* and *Google analytics*. If you are not confident in this area seek assistance from within your contact network and check out tutorials on YouTube.

21. MARKET INWARDS

How it Works

The sale of your product to the potential customer works a lot better when you have all customer-focused people on board. This can include customer centre staff, shop staff, distributors, suppliers, IT personnel and any others responsible for delivering value to the potential customer. Your existing customers can fall into this group. Marketing inwards means selling internally so that everybody is on board, knows what's going on and can act accordingly.

What to Do

To accomplish this, design an internal marketing campaign to run along side your external campaign. Start by getting buy-in from all appropriate parties early in the campaign design. Arrange a presentation that can cover the marketing campaign objectives, target audience, the offering, key marketing activities, campaign timeline and rewards for sales completed.

Keep your presentation concise and to the point. Others might not be as deeply excited about it as you. Give them the short summary. Your task is to educate and motivate frontline individuals to sell your offering to the customers, not to bore them or to frighten them into thinking you are doubling the workload.

Tips and Take Homes

Create promotion material only for the internal marketing with visual graphics that you can use to promote the rewards. Use this to share campaign success indicators through your internal communication such as emails and posters placed in employee areas.

Digital Nugget

Set up an internal online group where all involved can express their thoughts, wins and losses on the campaign. Here, you could have a simple live target metric for all to share and see. Encourage everyone to get involved by creating rewards for the most sales achieved or a collective reward of a paid night out if the team as a unit hit an agreed target.

22. CREATE BUYER PERSONAS

How it Works

Shape the personality of your brand by creating buyer personas. Buyer personas are fictional characters made to represent your collective customer base. These are the different types of customers that might purchase your product, visit your website or buy into your brand. Creating buyer personas enables you to speak your customers' language and be familiar with their buying patterns. It helps you to more strategically target your market leading to a better quality of leads and a higher percentage of customer retention. Buyer persona builds a template for you to produce compelling content geared towards different audiences with targeted offers. It is a method that will empower you to communicate with a large amount of people with one consistent voice.

What to Do

Establish the identity of your key buyers. Use customer surveys to research and define the average demographic segmentation. Focus on aspects such as age, gender, family size, disposable income and spending patterns. Although the persona is fictional, it's important not to invent it. For it to have true value it needs to be developed with facts and data that represent your customers. Go out and talk to people about your products. Talk to both your existing customers and your prospective clients. Once you have outlined your personas, authenticate them with people in the know, such as your sales team, customers and employees. Determine what you want to learn about your customers and prospects. Sift through your findings and find patterns. If you have transactional or other useful data, look at that too. Construct 2 or 3 personas that represent your customers. Use the personas to create the voice for your promotional marketing material. This will help you create better quality online content. It will help create the language used in all communication with your customers. This way they can get accustomed to your manner of interacting with them. Give the personas names. Make them real.

Tips and Take Homes

Be inspired by the process of creating the persona. Write a description of your personas from the first, second and third person to give you an idea of the type of language you wish to use.

Update your buyer personas regularly. Outside influences such as the economic climate and new emerging technologies will cause your customers to change. Your business will also change as it grows. Allow this to be reflected in your buyer personas by reviewing and updating them once or twice a year.

Digital Nugget

Dig deeper into your buyer personas by creating separate landing pages on your website for the different persona. This way they are arriving at a page that speaks directly to their needs. Here, you can test different calls to actions on different persona profiles.

23. WRITE A GREAT MARKETING CASE STUDY

How it Works

While it's always important to face your marketing plan head-on with a step-by-step view, imagine being able to see it from the end back to the start. One way to do this and avoid pitfalls is to write a successful marketing case study before it happens. Imagine your plan has been implemented and is now over: What would the real success story be? This exercise will create confidence and clarity in planning your campaign. It will give you ideas to implement that you may not think of when looking ahead.

What to Do

This is a fun exercise to help you paint a picture of what your marketing efforts will really achieve. What would a case study of your marketing success look like and how would it read? Write it! Write it as if it has already happened. Question every detail. If you state that you had record sales, ask why? Question your answers by creating different scenarios. Don't write a novel. Keep it short with an introduction stating the campaign target, timeline, tactics used and results. Then go into the detail. What you did, why it worked and what you learned. Cover all possible angles. Think about the market response. Think about the competition's reaction. Think about high demand. Can you handle it? Think about low demand? What's plan B and plan C?

Tips and Take Homes

Give focus to the profit and loss, your cost per customer acquisition and how changing situations impact on your budget. Look at customer depletion, as this is also a cost.

Digital Nugget

Once your real campaign is actually over, publish a real marketing case study along with your case study of predicted measures side by side on a blog post. Outline the things you got 'bang on' and point out the places where you were miles off.

24. IDENTIFY YOUR TRUE VALUE PROPOSITION

How it Works

Your true value proposition (TVP) is a strong statement of the real results that your customers get from using your products. Your TVP is not always what you think it is or what you want it to be. Actually, you may not have a say in it. The source must be unbiased. If you create a value proposition that does not match the product user perception and expectation, you will end up targeting the wrong market with the wrong message and limit your opportunity.

What to Do

Listen to your customers. Pay special attention to why they buy from you. If they are not communicating this to you, reach out and ask them. Don't try to manipulate or coach them into giving you your dream answer. Your TVP is what the majority of your customers think about you, say about you and the reason they use your product. You may not agree with it, but it is the best starting point for you to create conversation with your customers and potential customers. You may believe you have a great quality product that should be perceived in a certain light. Your customers, on the other hand, may use your product because it's perceived as cool, high end, low end, the only show in town, great customer service or simply cheap and cheerful. It's difficult to come up with a value proposition automatically. The best TVP's are grown spontaneously from existing customers. They are then captured and communicated to potential customers. Tell your potential customers that you are different from all the other companies because you don't just give a value proposition; you give a true value proposition created not by you, but by users.

Tips and Take Homes

A great TVP is an organic communication that keeps changing as the customer's behaviour and expectations change. When you capture your TVP regularly you can take advantage of the real time feelings customers have on the value your product brings to their experience. Add these phrases and words that make up your TVP to your communication. Keep it current and updated.

Digital Nugget

Create a platform whereby you capture your customer's thoughts on your service. The City Bin Co. created the 'Wall of Wows!' page online. This is where we post and share emails, comments, post and snail-mails from customers who say why they like to use our service. They say we are 'progressive', 'cool' and 'innovative'. They say, The City Bin Co. is the Google of the waste industry. They tell us we have great customer service and friendly staff. We then post these Wows to all of our social media platforms which generates more feedback online and reinforces the TVP of the company.

25. CRAFT A UNIQUE SELLING PROPOSITION

How it Works

Every business will say that they have a unique selling proposition (USP). A USP differentiates a product from that of its competitors, such as the lowest cost or the highest quality. It's what you have that your competitors don't. The word unique implies that it is original and found only with you. It is no longer a unique selling proposition if your competitors are singing the same song. It is just a bog standard selling proposition that you can get from any Joe Soap. Make the difference by digging deeper and taking ownership of a USP so that if anybody else states your USP, they will essentially be advertising your brand for you.

What to Do

To craft a great USP, you have to think like your customer. Understand what motivates your customer's purchasing choices. Identify the real reasons customers come to you instead of the rival companies. Look for what makes your business unique and valuable to your potential market. What do you do that nobody else does? Define your business objectives in one or two lines. Incorporate your USP into your company slogan or tagline reinforcing your uniqueness. Keep your USP short. Make sure it is consistent. Highlight the potential emotional satisfaction.

Tips and Take Homes

Your USP is different from your TVP. Your USP is created by you and defines the one thing that makes your business special and different from every other business with a similar offering. You will tell your potential customer your USP in order to persuade them to buy. A TVP is created by the customers and framed by you after they have used your product. This states the true reasons why they use your product. Knowing your TVP will help you structure your USP.

Digital Nugget

Promote your USP digitally using video. Produce short clips that bring your USP to life with sight, sound and action.

26. GET INTIMATE WITH YOUR CUSTOMERS

How it Works

Surveys are a great way to research your customer base. You can get honest feedback on issues such as service, pricing, and quality. The information you receive will help you develop a sense of how customers rate you. It will give you a good indication of where you need to improve. You will learn the problems that customers are having with your products. This will give you a chance to re-engage with your customers when you address those problems. You will also get an opportunity to see who are the customers that will champion your brand.

What to Do

The City Bin Co. has tried and tested many means of surveying customers and brand research over the years. We start with our customers and we listen to them. We learn from our customers and we communicate with them regularly. Our main emphasis is on customer service. The City Bin Co. has adopted the Net Promoter Score (NPS) as the method of measuring customer satisfaction through the consistent customer surveying. This technique, founded by Bain Consulting is the preferred method across Fortune 1000 companies. In fact, over 60 percent of the world's top 2,000 companies use NPS to track customer satisfaction and loyalty. The system managed by *Satmetrix* measures some of the world's leading companies such as Amazon, Hertz and Nike.

NPS scores companies on a scale of -100 to 100. A positive mark is a good score and the global average is 15. An exceptional score is 50. The City Bin Co. scores consistently above the 70 mark. This places The City Bin Co. in the top 5 percent of companies globally alongside such giants as Apple, Virgin, and Google. It places The City Bin Co. as one of the top Irish names in the system. We are a 100 per cent customer-centric company. We are in the business of delivering a first-rate service to our customers and everything we do is based on that. This real-time benchmark helps us to shape our marketing strategies on a continuous basis. We are better informed to tell and share our brand story on the right platforms, in turn, building strong brand awareness and connections through authentic customer experiences.

Find out what system or survey provider will suit your needs. Get intimate with your customers by asking questions. Ask questions to find out how much they care about your product or your brand. Ask questions about their experience from beginning to end with your company and your product. Find out where they would like you to improve. Ask if they would recommend your business or products to a friend. Do your surveys through a third party to keep everything transparent and authentic?

Tips and Take Homes

The beauty of the NPS is that you only ask one question. People, in general, are busy and do not like to feel hassled by businesses. No matter what platform you use to survey your customers, keep it brief. Figure out the most important piece of information you are interested in acquiring and go ask it.

Digital Nugget

Well-planned surveys will return useful data about who cares enough to talk about your product. Using systems such as the NPS will enable you to see the ideal promoters of your brand and product. Invite them to record a video blog or contribute a short sound bite for your product that can be shared across your social media platforms.

27. MIND THE MONEY: MARKETING BUDGET

How it Works

The best marketing campaigns keep an eye on the budget and give a healthy return for their investment. Going over budget is not an option when it comes to your marketing spend unless you have a money tree planted in your garden. Make a price plan and use it as a guideline.. Don't add to it because an agency tells you it would be great to get X,Y and Z and it will enhance the campaign. If anything, look at what you don't need as opposed to what you need.

Failure to properly look at your cost or budget your marketing plan could lead to problems. Insufficient funding for such items as equipment or staff can become unwanted headaches for the whole business. It is the lack of a suitably-constructed marketing budget that dooms many marketing plans and campaigns. A marketing budget is the marketing plan written in terms of costs.

What to Do

Create a list of all the diverse parts of your marketing plan such as research, product testing and production of promotional material. Work out the potential costs of the overall marketing campaign. Think of the costs of design for packaging, adverts online and offline and websites. Work out your budget for media such as outdoor bilboards, leaflet drops, TV and radio commercials. Plan your marketing budget to verify that your strategy is strong in terms of cost. Look back over your spend and success during previous marketing campaigns. This will help make informed calculations. Do a case-study. Research past competitor campaigns and similiar marketing ventures for a ballpark cost idea. Budget for all your commitments. Know where there is a large spend. Ask for a contract of commitment on fixed cost. Ask the media to take half the cost risk if an agreed target is not met in your campaign.

Tips and Take Homes

When it comes to creating a spend strategy for your marketing campaign, hold back a minimum reserve of 10 percent for emergency resources. If the plan is not working or if your competitor reacts, you will have finances to call on if needed. Also, team up and combine your marketing skills with those of an accountant to make sure that the numbers add up. You need to know that the overall spend and predicted return is realistic.

Digital Nugget

Drive all sales through a web-based platform. This way, you can measure and link the marketing spend directly to your sales. If you have a limited budget for marketing start with the 'zero to low cost' items such as planning and forecasting. Write press releases, take photographs and make introduction videos. Start small and grow. No need to take over the world over night! Build the brand one block at a time. Contact the local media and get them on board. Create a buzz through word of mouth marketing.

USE DIGITAL MARKETING WITH CONFIDENCE

Digital marketing is neither a 'jump-on' bandwagon nor the latest fad in the business world. It is part of the new business landscape that gives you a great set of marketing tools. They are available for you to use and can help to increase your sales. Technology is here to stay so you need to embrace it. Get somebody who is confident in that area to show you the basics if you feel it's out of your comfort-zone. In 1999, my younger brother, Ronan, had designed and created his own website at the age of 11. My children who are now under the age of 5 know their way around tablets and touchscreen technology. They can open apps and find their favourite cartoon on YouTube. My smart television has not caught up as the kids always try to change the channel daily by swiping the screen with their fingers; I am sure that it's only a matter of time.

Digital marketing is very much part of everyday life. It is growing as an essential tool in the consumer's life and everyday business. You don't need to be an expert in digital marketing, but you can become confident in the digital sphere in a short timeframe. Practice and persistence is key. If you don't know how to do something look on YouTube for online tutorials. This is a new world with new rules that can enhance your sales. Digital marketing has levelled the playing field in giving all businesses access to affordable tools that give a wider reach.

Traditionally, the customer had to physically go into the business space to make a purchase. Now, the business can go to the potential customer space to make a sale. A small company would have trouble reaching the same marketing reach of a bigger or more experienced competitor with traditional marketing practices alone. Digital marketing has given a worldwide audience to all businesses who wish to grow their sales no matter what the size, which would have been near to impossible if you were only using traditional marketing.

Digital marketing changes the game by creating equal opportunities for all business and all consumers. Digital marketing enables you to measure and analyse numbers in real time. This empowers you to adjust your marketing strategy to achieve maximum results. When it comes to digital marketing don't ignore it, explore it and exploit it to your advantage.

28. BE A CLICK AWAY FROM GOING GLOBAL

How it Works

There is no such thing as local, national or international anymore. Nowadays, every business has the ability to be a click away from global. You may not have a global business yet, but your reach can be global using today's vast and free online social media platforms. You can be a local business with a global network. When you sell your product and tell your story to get new clients, you can have a worldwide reach. I was amazed when I got my first book order from Ian Elliot at the 'Different Drummer' bookstore in Ontario, Canada as I was only promoting in Ireland at the time. It was my first lesson in selling on the world stage. A customer of Ian's had seen an article about my first book 'The Binman's Guide to Selling' in *CEOworld*, an online business magazine, and went to his local store to order a copy of my book.

What to Do

Set up online and throw that net wide. If you are not selling outside a certain geographical zone, they can still be talking about you! If you can't service a certain area they can still be wearing your branded t-shirts and engaging with your story online. Reach for the stars by thinking beyond your local market. Become an online merchant. You have to position your business a few mouse clicks away from a global customer base. Start by setting up your website to receive orders and enquiries from other countries.

Tips and Take Homes

Start small. Investigate logistics. If your service or product is too difficult to transfer to other markets, move the brand and the expertise of the brand. The product will follow.

Digital Nugget

Set up an online forum for all users of your products, including your competitor's products within the industry. This allows you tap into the demands and needs of potential clients overseas. Crucially, include a merchant shop and there are many versions available.

29. GET SEO SAVVY

How it Works

Search Engine Optimization (SEO) is the practice of gaining top results for your webpage in online search engines. Having a website and keeping it a secret will not help you sell your products. In today's world of fast moving technology, the obligation is not just on the developer of the site to take responsibility for the search engine ranking; it's also on you. SEO means to optimise your website so that it achieves the highest possible organic search rankings on the different search engines in a natural algorithmic way. This is not a once-off event. This means a commitment to continuous engagement, tweaking and refinement. The bar is always rising and the systems are continuously changing. You are in control of your website's positioning. You can control this by focusing on content, meta-tags, keywords and link building. If you are not tech savvy you will need help from a SEO expert to implement your strategy. Make sure your website is mobile friendly as this also has an influence your SEO ranking.

What to Do

Get SEO Savvy! Understand the way it works. Understand what you can do and what is best left to the experts. Search engines use algorithms to measure the importance of a website and its content to a search term. They constantly evaluate websites by looking at the quality and freshness of content, overall completeness of page threads, the site's credibility and the reliability of information provided. Before you begin, you must know where you are.

Perform a website SEO audit that will check where you stand in SEO ranking. Generally, they will look at the quality of meta-tags, titles, descriptions, keywords, links and visibility. This can be done with the assistance of a web specialist: there are good free online tools that will give you a basic report. Just go to a search engine and type 'Free website audit.' There are 3 areas you can be proactive in a systematic manner that will influence your SEO. They are:

1. Content building
2. Blogging
3. Link Building

Be effective in creating good content for activities that you can share on social media sites. Do it habitually. Reach out and ask to be invited as a guest blogger on high-ranking sites with influence in your industry. Most importantly, start link building. Link building is the practice of generating links to your website from elsewhere on the internet. Links pointing to your content are strong indicators in the search engines' valuation of your site. It tells the search engine that all these high quality sites are pointing at you. Developing good SEO results takes time, so give it time.

Tips and Take Homes

There is a big difference between organic SEO results and paid SEO results. If you are looking to use advert campaigns to improve your SEO ranking, be aware that as soon as you stop paying, you stop being seen. If you get it right naturally you will not have to pay dearly. The goal is to appear in the first page of the search engine which people look for your company name and keywords related to your products, business and industry. You need to own this page. Start by making product videos and posting them on the different social media channels. Find bloggers and other businesses who blog about topics related to your industry and ask them to link their page back to you. When you do this you are simply showing the search engine that other websites are pointing at your page. This gives the search engine a good indication that your page is relevant to others and therefore pushes you up the search ranking.

Digital Nugget

The search engine companies already make it easy and have dozens of tools to help your website perform well. Register *Google Webmaster Tools* and make sure you have *Google Analytic's* code added to your website.

30. USE THE RIGHT SOCIAL MEDIA CHANNELS

What to Do

Social media is exactly what it says on the tin. It's social and it's media. And it's fun! The best way to grow your business in this space is to pick one or two suitable platforms and be committed 100% to being the best at them. Take Facebook: too many business pages are a) not business pages, but personal pages b) not updated or c) non-existent. Social media brings ample opportunities to connect and communicate with existing and future customers. There are different social media channels out there and more and more coming on stream. You don't have to be on them all. There are two different types of social media sites: 1) The fast moving ones where you post content & communicate with followers in real time such as Facebook and Twitter and 2) the media sites where you create and store content such as YouTube or a blog which can act like an online newsletter. Many years ago, before the internet came into our lives, a lot of business people would have paid a lot of money to be a fly on the wall and know exactly what customers and potential customers were thinking and saying about their business and products. They would have loved to know if the words spoken were negative or positive and how many people were talking about them and what they said about the quality of the products. That day has now arrived and it's called social media. The cost of use is between minimal and free but the value is only redeemable if used correctly and creatively by the user.

How it Works

Don't just have one foot in and the other out. Be committed to building a carefully selected and manageable amount of social channels. Fill them with rich material so that when your clients arrive on your social channels they are met with engaging content. Create a yearly content calendar that will guide you to post regularly. When you are thinking about what to talk about, think social. If you met these people out and about you wouldn't just talk about your products all the time. Talk about the community, the weather or the next *Hallmark* day. Turn your words into pictures or videos where possible. It's much easier for somebody to respond to a picture or click 'play' than read a body of text. Invite them to post their thoughts about all these topics and your business on your page and interact with them.

Tips and Take Homes

Answer your comments and posts ASAP. No matter what kind of comment you receive in your social media space, always take action to answer it as soon as possible. Never ignore a comment. If the comment is positive, thank them for their kind words. Repost it on your other social media platforms. It's a testimonial! If a comment is negative towards your product, answer it too. Stand up for what you believe in. If a phone was ringing in your office you wouldn't just stare at it and think 'I will answer it next week' and if somebody was to call with a complaint you would do your best to resolve any issues as soon as humanly possible. With the availability of smart phones and apps to support these social media sites I believe most comments can be answered in real time. That's what makes it social. That's why it works well when it's used well. If comments and posts are left unanswered, this can leave a negative impression. How people see you online will build an impression of how they believe you are offline. The days of nine to five are gone. Social media has turned sales and customer service into a 24 hour a day one stop shop, put a system in place that allows you to respond if you get a tweet, comment, message or post out of hours.

Digital Nugget

All these platforms are businesses that wish to sell you their product. Use the free packages and you will get minimum results. There are exceptions, but those are few and far between. Pay to post adverts and boost content and you will see an increase in activity.

31. BE THE STEVEN SPIELBERG FOR YOUR COMPANY

How it Works

They say a picture is worth a thousand words. A video clip can be worth a million and much more. When The City Bin Co. took the decision to enter the wonderful world of social media one of the stumbling blocks we faced was with YouTube. When you did a search on YouTube for The City Bin Co. you would get pages upon pages of results with video after video of Bin Laden. This was because of the word *bin*. The task was to take ownership of our brand name on the video platforms and the only way to do that was to make videos. In the first year we made over one hundred videos for our YouTube Channel and had over 40,000 views. Mr. Bin Laden took a back seat in the search engine. We learned the power of a video. We learned what it meant to our customers. Our sales and marketing team used the videos as tools to explain our offerings. When you are making videos you are creating content that can be shared over and over again.

What to Do

The first step is to buy a video-dedicated high definition camera and use it! You are aiming to translate your business and products into short videos. Use video to demystify your product. Make it easy to understand your product and ultimately make a sale or support a sale. The trick with video marketing is as follows: Don't make one video. Just keep making them. Why? The more you make the better you get at it. The more videos you upload the more views you get which means you can drive more traffic to your website.

When you have potential customers in your online virtual store you have to keep them interested. It's so much easier for them to hit the play button than read a mountain of text. Plan your videos. Plan their content by creating a pre video production list. Start by writing down 20 possible ideas and titles. Create storyboards with quick sketches. Use the platform to express ideas such as brand stories, video podcasts, how to use the product, product overviews, frequently asked questions, client case studies, meet the team, and what customers are saying. You must take ownership of your company channel. Be the Steven Spielberg for your brand. Make videos that will support your sales team and their goals.

Tips and Take Homes

Don't worry about not being a professional video maker. Online videos tend to be watched more when they have a 'fly on the wall' feel to the production. You can learn by watching what others do and don't do. To get ideas and inspiration watch clips by companies and people from all industries. Keep your videos short. Between 30 seconds to a minute and a half is what I recommend. Put your key message first. If somebody clicks on another video or goes off your page, be sure they got your message. Invest in a cinematic animation of your company logo that you can use at the end of each video. Share videos by email to your customers. Don't just make videos and use them online where they will fade over time into the background. Use the videos offline for store video displays and product presentations. In order to get maximum results from your video, work on an effective video message. Ask the following questions of each video: Is it creative? Is it informative? Is it entertaining? When the video is made, edited and posted to its final destination measure the results. Don't just measure the views, measure how many sales you got from your video. This will give you a point to start from and improve on.

Digital Nugget

Videos are something you can do and edit yourself; I encourage you to make one professional video for your website. Let this be your introduction video that explains who you are, what you do, why you do it and how you can help. People who visit webpages with videos tend to stay longer on that page. And those who stay longer on websites will take more of an interest in buying your product.

32. PRODUCE A PERFECT POST PLANNER

How it Works

Planning and preparation is key to success in social media. Most businesses struggle with content creation for online platforms. The audience is there, the business is there and nobody is connecting. It's as if you are gagged and nobody is paying much attention to you. If you are not saying the right things people will switch off fast. First rule to remember is that it's a *social* network, not a *spam* network. The second thing to clarify is the purpose of your online platforms. Is it to build brand awareness? Is it to create a sales channel? Or is it to provide customer service? Is it to build relationships? The City Bin Co. uses social media as an important source for customer support as it is becoming a daily first point of contact for customers to voice their praises, grumbles and queries. By responding and interacting with our customers to answer their questions, we are building trust and brand awareness. This helps to boost engagement. It also allows us to be available in our customers' space.

What to Do

Focus on the goals you wish to achieve by taking a systematic approach when creating a content calendar for your company. First of all think about the audience you are speaking to and why would they engage with you? Decide on the tone and message of your posts. Use mixed mediums to deliver your messages such as video, photos, blogs, pictures with quotes and links. Design content around key days in your industry or key events within your community. Celebrate important holidays and festivals in your area. Use a weekly post planner with daily posts to ensure your content is strong and consistent. For example on Facebook start with the *Monday Marketing Memorabilia,* then a *Tuesday Blog Post, Wednesday's Creative Pic, Throwback Thursday*, and end the week with *Funny Friday!* After this, create posts around your work environment, birthday celebrations, local events and holidays.

This will allow you to have a high quality engagement from both customers and potential clients. Create a content calendar annually and reviewed on an ongoing basis. In planning your content, you create an opportunity to chat to your potential clients as if you were having a chat over a coffee. The best way to be there successfully is to plan the post so you show up on time speaking with a human tone about human things.

Tips and Take Homes

When you create a content calendar for your company, you have a document that can be used to plan all content marketing activity. Make this document accessible to all in your company that may need to see it. Delegate the tasks if you can't look after updates or content schedules. The advantage of using the post planner is that you can envisage how your content is flowing throughout the year. Also, always have back up content like a blog piece or photos in case you need to post something out of the blue!

Digital Nugget

Create links where possible on your blogs and on your videos. Create a page on your website that pulls your top and must recent content from all of your different social media channels on to your website. Don't just settle for the small social media button style icons. Let your social media own some real space on your homepage. The City Bin Co. give a big percentage of their website's homepage over to the blog, youtube video and facebook.

33. CREATE A KEYWORD STRATEGY

How it Works

Keyword Strategy is all about being easily found. It's about being ranked in the top of search engine results. When you create a keyword strategy, you are making it easier for your potential customers to find you. You are essentially creating a small collection of keywords applicable to your business and helping your potential customers find you. You are putting a virtual tracker on your product or business. If your website is your online shop, your keywords are your doorbell. You are also telling the online search engines when somebody is looking for these keywords to send them to this website. It is the first step in your overall marketing strategy as it is an exercise that will shape the feel and tone of how you communicate with your clients. When you find the keywords that work for you, incorporate them into the copy for all your online communication on social media, blogs, and mirco-sites. This will help you to create your unique identity as perceived by the public.

What to Do

Start from scratch and have a brainstorming meeting with an objective to create a list of keywords applicable to your business. Keep the list short and relevant with a maximum of 5 to 10 words. Focus on the language your customers use when speaking about your business and not just the words you would like associated with your business. Put yourself in your customer's shoes. Invite one or two customers to be part of the meeting. Ask them about the terms they use when searching for your product online. What words do people use when looking for your products? Keywords are not about your product name or brand name but more about the action the potential client needs to fulfill; for example: your target audience will look for a *'bin collection for South West London'* instead of a named brand or product in the industry. Use online keyword builders to generate a list of words applicable to your industry.

Tips and Take Homes

Nothing is set in stone when it comes to keywords. Using the right keywords in a competitive environment that does not always work. Your message can get lost in a sea of companies all shouting the same thing. You need to think of keywords in the area of competitiveness, product relativity and brand uniqueness.

Create keywords specifically for certain content and individual landing pages. Test different groups of keywords on different landing pages to see which perform better.

Digital Nugget

Keywords that don't work must walk the plank. Don't be precious about words you want to associate with you brand. If it's not performing be prepared to chop and change and to do this successfully you need to measure the performance of the keywords.

34. WIN NEW CUSTOMERS WITH WEBINARS

How it Works

Hosting a webinar is an energetic and engaging way to economically communicate with a wide audience. You can organise an online event that is hosted by your company. You can broadcast to a target group of prospective clients or existing customers. Webinars are also known as webcasts or online seminars. They allow you to share a topic-focused presentation using videos, web pages, slides, your desktop and other multimedia content. The audience can be located anywhere in the world. The visual component of a webinar is shared through a third party web conferencing tool or Internet browser. The audio portion of a webinar is usually broadcast through the speakers on attendees' computers. The presentation is almost always followed up with a questions and answers session or a call to action. Webinars are also used for real time surveys. It's a great way to interact and communicate your message with an audience. Once a webinar is complete, it makes great content for sharing on your social media platforms.

What to Do

Choose a topic that can benefit your potential client and address their needs. It does not have to relate to your product or company. The first webinar I ever did was with Ann Halloran of In-Tuition, a company that helps businesses set up online. Ann interviewed me on 'How to create a successful social media plan.' It had nothing to do with the product or the company where I work. It was offering solid advice to our potential clients and their needs. Over 200 business people signed up for that webinar with attendees joining us globally from Mexico to Australia. I could map out my book sales from that webinar to the locations of the audience. I never mentioned the book once. Nothing turns off an audience faster than a direct sales pitch, which is almost always easy to identify. The tone changes, from teaching to selling. Plan your webinar from start to finish. Your only interest should be to share information. In exchange for that information, you are asking them to share their details and asking them to share the content with their database. In other words, you are spreading the brand name and positioning you and your business as a go-to person in the area of your expertise. The sale happens in the follow up. Plan the content of your webinar. Rehearse it over and over.

Do a dummy run before the webinar. This will give you time to practice. You can pre record it so that you have a good idea of how it will look and sound. Use real time surveys during the webinar. This will give it an interactive element that gives ownership of the content to the attendees. If you are planning on doing a few webinars invite experts to be interviewed on topics that will be of interest to your potential attendees. This adds variety.

When you are ready, send out the invites to your customers and potential customers. Send a few personal e-mail invites to people on your radar who you feel would have a real interest in the topic. Allow plenty of time for the questions and answers. If there is a question you can't answer in that moment or a question that brings you into an area you don't wish to talk about, you can answer by saying:

'John, that's a great question. I will answer you via email as I might have a link or two I can share with you.'

Mary, Thank you kindly for your question. I won't answer that today as it doesn't relate to the topic or theme of the webinar; however, I will drop you an email with some information you may find interesting.'

Always acknowledge the attendee's question and close it off. If you can't help them there and then, do it via email after the event. They will appreciate the follow up. When closing off the webinar, let your audience know when your next webinar will be and the topic. Ask them to invite a friend or their clients.

Tips and Take Homes

Your aim is for the audience to identify with you as the presenter and the product that you represent without visually spamming them. You are simply creating a virtual hub through which you can support potential clients with whom you can build rapport. People generally go to webinars because they want to learn something, not to buy something. Place the webinar into your company's sales funnel as a means of qualifying prospects. Build a platform that they can come back to again and again to learn more. When you keep their attention they will do the homework and see what else you have to offer. Webinars are also a great support tool for sharing tips and tricks for better user experience and product maintenance.

Digital Nugget

Send out a feedback survey to the attendees after each webinar. Ask them what they liked and what they learned from it. Ask them if there is anything that they would change or add. Ask them to rate the webinar out of ten. Send all attendees a link of the recorded webinar a week after. This acts as a refresher of their experience and a reminder for the next webinar.

35. START EMAIL MARKETING NOW

How it Works

When you send an email the first thing you want the recipient to think is, *'I got mail'* and not, *'I'm being spammed.'* Email marketing is targeting a lot of people at a particular time with a clear message and desired content. The audience must be the right audience. The time must be relevant to the content and convenient for those who receive it. The content must be engaging. Email marketing is one of the most effective tools for delivering appropriate and appealing content to a large audience. Email is the first thing people check when they arrive at work each morning. Even when out of work, you are checking your professional and personal email as technology has made it so easy and accessible. The goal of email marketing is to touch base with a client or potential client, boost brand awareness and help sell your services.

When new customers sign up to The City Bin Co.'s service online, they receive an email message from the CEO of the company welcoming them to the service. Embedded in the email is a short video of the CEO and managing director telling the exciting story explaining why the company was set up. After this, they receive a detailed and colourful report on their recycling behaviours once a month. This report is called a bindex. This is an informative communication that helps customers make good recycling choices. On the run up to Christmas 2013, we sent over 40,000 customers an e-mail with 3 vouchers as a *'thank you'* for being our customer. One of the vouchers was for a local toy company, My Toys Direct. Another voucher came from a ham company, Brady's Irish Ham and the third one from Easons, Ireland's biggest bookshop. Again, the timing was important and the content was relevant and engaging.

The best people to target are the ones who have willingly signed up to receive emails from you, who want it and who expect it. These are normally already your customers. When you start thinking of email marketing as a relationship builder and not a product pusher, you will get results. It's not something you do once and do big. It's a process to be developed over time with a view to creating recurring positive touch points with clients and potential clients through the process of email. You can easily and quickly reach target markets for very little cost. The impact can be immediate and measurable.

What to Do

In order to get your email marketing on full throttle, the first step is to create your email database or list. It is important that you investigate the relevant data protection laws in your country and abide by them. Start by putting a procedure in place where you give every customer and person with an interest in your service an opportunity to sign up to receive emails from your company. If you have a subscribe option on your website or in your sales funnel be sure to keep it as simple as possible. Only ask for an email and a name. People generally don't like filling out forms. Be clear as to what they are signing up to. On my Binman's Guide website, I ask only for an email and I state clearly 'Sign up for Oisin's Free E-Book Download, Famous Non-Newsletter, Business Insights & Inspirations!' Offer something such as a whitepaper or a tip sheet on an appropriate topic if they sign up. Give a little to receive a little.

Always give the option to unsubscribe and make it equally easy to do so. There is no sense in talking to people who have no interest in what you are saying. It's better to have 100 quality email contacts in your database than 10,000 receivers who don't want your email. Design an email marketing strategy around your business and what you could best communicate in the emails. Your aim is to build engaging content to strengthen relationships and interact with your potential customers and existing clients. Email marketing can carry 3 main functions: attractive offers, great content and informative tools that build your relationship and your client base. How often will you communicate by email? What will this communication look like? Who will receive it and what do you want the response to be?

When Fabienne, owner of La Rouge, a French Restaurant based in the West of Ireland, sat down to discuss her marketing plan we came up with an idea that filled her restaurant every night. Fabienne printed beautiful *'rate your plate'* cards with only one question: Can you rate your plate between 1 and 5. Underneath this was a request for an email address with a little box to be ticked and a line stating, *'If you would like to receive promotional material via email please tick here.'* The postcard also had a monthly competition for those who subscribed. When the customer requested the bill, Fabienne would bring all the guests a *'Rate My Plate'* card and ask them to fill them out. Once a month she would announce the winner via email and invite them for a prize of a 3-course meal for 2 on the house. Everybody else on her email list would receive runner up vouchers that could be used on certain nights.

The restaurant was always booked out. Through this process Fabienne was giving a great offer that resulted in repeat business. She shared the ratings and information collected from her clients with them all collectively and offered discounts on her quieter nights to the customers who took part.

Tips and Take Homes

Design an email template that is easy to read, straight to the point and is consistent with your brand. Make the experience easy for the reader. Where possible send emails based on specific user actions as is in case of The City Bin Co. when the customer signs up for the first time they get a welcome email. Think of Fabienne in the French Restaurant: You were never going to get an email from her if you didn't eat in her eatery. Think about your subject line and the message you want to have there. If the reader never opens your email what one thing will they get from the title of your message? Learn how to setup conversion tracking. Use it for your email marketing so you can get real time data on your email campaigns in relation to emails opened, emails clicked through and conversions.

Digital Nugget

Build your email list with quality contacts that wish to hear from you. Start with the already converted: your loyal customers. Always give an opt-in and an opt-out option.

Share any positive results or feedback on your website so potential customers see the positive ratings of your current clients.

36. BUILD FOR MOBILE VIEWING

How it Works

In the world of technology the touch points where your customers look for you are changing. Devices such as smartphones and tablets have fast become the number one point of contact between you and your content viewer.

When creating any online platform such as a website or a blog the best place to start is with the user. Think about the tools they will be using to access your content. It is important to have an interactive website that is built to conform to individual devices. If your potential customers are accessing information published by you and your company, you want what they see to be presentable and easy to navigate. You do not want to lose them. They may not be viewing what you have to offer on a desktop. Consumers care about their experience, regardless of how you deliver it. They care that it works on their device no matter what device they are using. They care that it allows them to get what they need. They even care about how fast your page loads. When you build everything for mobile viewing and keep up with your customers' buying habits you help with their basic needs. Mobile viewing is not just about providing a great customer experience; it is the new customer expectation.

What to Do

If you don't have a website or you are at a point where you are ready to upgrade your online portal, work from the viewpoint of being mobile and responsive. Create a website that easily enables people to stay on your site and navigate with ease. If there is one action you want everybody who enters your site to do, what is it? What do you need to give them to get there? Think about the video content. The length of the videos on your site can upset a user experience. What message do you need to convey? They may check you out on their mobile and make an informed decision to buy in store or online based on what they see.

The mobile user is not sitting down to go through your site for fun. They are either looking for something or you have invited them to see something. Make it quick and to the point.

Tips and Take Homes

Think of your customers' online behaviour. Track the patterns of user behaviour on your current site. Let this inform your decision in relation to the placement of content and the order of pages on your site.

Digital Nugget

Don't show huge amounts of data if their screen is small. Don't overload them with useless information, which can slow down their ability to find what they want. Give the important information first. Keep the mobile viewing simple so that people can find what they are looking for quickly and have a link that allows the user to visit the main website from the mobile.

37. BLOG FOR YOUR CUSTOMERS

How it Works

Business blogs are powerful marketing and communication tools. They help companies to communicate better with customers, potential clients and associates. Blogs are great relationship builders that enable the human side of the business to shine. As most blogs are updated regularly and rich with keywords, it will help you to gain good search engine optimised results for your products and business. A blog is only as good as the content you publish. The consistency of your posts, the views and the response from the audience are all key indicators of a good blog. A blog sits in its own unique social space online. Think of your blog as the newsroom and all your social media platforms such as Facebook, Twitter and LinkedIn as your distinctive channels. The newsroom is where you put the content together and the channels are where you distribute them out to the different audiences. Your blog represents your company and speaks to your audience without selling. It's the digital newsletter.

What to Do

There are a lot of easy to use online tools such as *Blogger* and *Wordpress* where you can be blogging in no time. A blog built into your website is always the best option as it keeps the reader in your virtual shop. A well set-up business blog has a structure where it is easy for the user to know where he is and what he can expect. Your audience needs to know what to expect. When you arrive at The City Bin Co.'s blog 'The Flying Bin' the first thing you read is a short blurb on what you can expect to find in the blog:

'Welcome to The City Bin Co.'s official blog where we keep it social and fun! We share hints and tips on customer service and social media! Also, you will find our winning at binning moments and interviews with our super customer centre team. Enjoy!

Focus on a particular subject matter and a series of topics where your potential clients may have an interest. Title all blog posts with a hook that makes the reader want to know more. For example: *What Price tag has 'Customer Experience' and what return?* Or *Learn The Top 5 Reasons Why You're Not Closing The Sale.* Hook them in with a question that they would like answered or a statement that makes them want to know more.

Challenge your audience with a statement that they may or may not agree with. Check out blogs of other businesses in your industry. Start responding to them and linking them to applicable articles in your blog. Typically, your blogs should be between 100 to 200 words. A professional picture should accompany them. Include links to videos and other informative sites that are relevant to your blog post. Aim to have sharable content.

If you are operating within the B2B market you can help your sales team close the sale by blogging about their prospects. Find out who are the top 5 commercial prospects in their pipeline. Write a post on your blog about their businesses. Share the top 3 reasons why they are a great business. Promote them. This becomes another tool in your sales team's toolbox.

Tips and Take Homes

Don't oversell on your blog. A link back to your main website will do. Have a picture of you or your company bloggers. This will add personality to the page. When you write and post a blog don't sit on it. Email it out to everybody and ask them to share, follow and comment on it. Invite guest bloggers to write a post for your blog. This will give a little bit of external perspective on your blog topics. It is a great way to gain new followers. Share the blog link through the different social media channels. Blogging is your opportunity to be the expert in your industry. Don't blog for your business; blog for your customers. Enlighten your customers with entertaining content that will cause them to engage. Connect with them by sharing success stories.

Digital Nugget

Make sure your blog contains an email subscription form. Blogging is one of the easiest ways to build your email database. To achieve this don't write just one blog. Push them out every week or every second week, whatever is suitable to your industry. Good, sharable quality posts shared frequently are what attracts the readers and creates excellent numbers.

38. BUILD A MOBILE APP

How it Works

The best apps are creative, simple and interactive. If you had an app for your business what would it look like and who would use it? To launch an app in today's business world is neither unusual nor rare, it's quite the norm. If you wish to pursue an app, do. Do it to be different. Offer an app that will make life easier for the user to have fun. Work out the benefits to your business and your customers. Write down the reasons why somebody would download your app and use it. An app should increase engagement with your customer, potential customers or other users. Think in terms of customer interactions and support.

What to Do

First thing to do is to research the market. See what apps are available that relate to your business sector. Speak to the developers and owners of these apps. See what they would do differently if they were to do it again. When you have an idea of the functions you wish your app to provide, simply draw it out on paper. Mock up a wireframe prototype before you pay big bucks to get it developed. This is really to create a visual of the app by means of simplified drawings or using basic app creation tools. This will give you a clear idea of the functionality of the app, its tone, and customer usability. If you believe it's a contender that adds value to your business, make it, launch it and promote it. It will allow you to plan the user journey.

Tips and Take Homes

Don't mimic the functions of your website. Do something that adds value to the service. You could create a nice tool that sends push notifications to customers after they make a purchase to update them with tips and techniques. Craft offers especially for the app users. Create a simple game, puzzle or educational tool that is linked to your brand. The app reach can be much wider than your existing customer base and potential client reach.

Digital Nugget

Use existing online channels to tell potential users that there is an easier way to communicate with your business. You should let them know you have an app. Convert your email and text communications over to push notifications driving your customers to download and use the app.

39. RECORD AN AMAZING PODCAST SERIES

How it Works

You no longer have to be a radio personality to reach the masses with your message. Recording a collection of podcasts gives you a fantastic way to share your voice, vision, views, and other interests. You can advertise your products or service. You can talk to your customers. You can be known as an authority on a given subject in your industry. You can build your own list of customers or your own fan base. My good friend, Jenny Brennan, of VOW, a social media and Facebook specialist, uses podcasting to increase her visibility by interviewing world-renowned experts in social media such as Mari Smith and Ian Carly. She starts out by emailing these experts and inviting them to be interviewed on her 'meet the expert' podcast series. The interview is then shared on Jenny's social media platforms and that of the person she is interviewing. This gives Jenny a broader reach. With the podcast as a springboard Jenny has now built personal and professional relationships with some of the experts that she has interviewed and is now seen as a leader on the social media world stage. Jenny uses podcasts to link up with global audiences. Through this, she has signed up international clients across the world for her virtual office business.

What to Do

Create your own radio style talk show. Interview the experts in your industry. Use *Skype* and a recording application such as *Screencast-O-Matic* to record and *YouTube* to upload your podcast. Before pressing the record button write out a list of questions that you can use to guide the interviews. Pick a hand full of experts you wish to speak to and send them an email inviting them to be interviewed. Think about the content of your podcast in terms of what problems you are solving. Launch the series. Ask your invited listeners and your interviewees to share the finished podcast.

Tips and Take Homes

Give your podcast series a catchy title that will resonate with your audience. A great example of this is Nathalie Nahai, author of *Webs of Influence: The Psychology of Online Persuasion*. Nathalie's podcast series is called; '*The good, the bad and the dirty secrets of persuasion.*'

Digital Nugget

Create a podcast page on your website where people may listen to old podcasts or make suggestions for people they would like to hear you interview. Provide a share button that makes it easy for the listener to share your contact on their social platforms.

40. SHARE THIRD PARTY CONTENT

How it Works

You can create and share content. Let's face it, there is enough content online. Creating content, although rewarding, is time consuming. If time is not on your side share the content already out there. Strike a healthy balance between sharing content important to your brand and creating in-house content that you feel is good enough for others to share on their social media sites.

What to Do

Become an expert content curator. Become a great collector. Think like a stamp or coin collector. Learn what information is of value or rare. Identify the themes around your brand, your vision and your culture. Maybe you are focused on customer service, or recycling or having fun. This will help provide the context. Collect links, pictures, videos and blog posts; share the best bits with your community. Deliver an evaluated assortment of the best, most applicable and interesting items on a very specific topic or theme that will almost look custom-made for your audience.

Tips and Take Homes

You have untapped resources right under your nose with your employees, suppliers and customers. Ask them to get involved in creating the biggest resource on a certain topic.

Digital Nugget

It is good practice to give credit and link back your curated content to the original web source. This gives your audience a chance to dig deeper into the content. It shows that you are being genuine. It tells the author of the material that you are endorsing them. Content curators are the greatest advocates for content creators. It shows that the work is worth sharing.

41. TURN YOUR WEBSITE INTO AN AUTOMATED SALES MACHINE

How it Works

Too many business websites are brochure sites with little to no interaction for the visitor to participate in. If your client has come to buy, your website needs to be lean and have no distractions. Don't overwhelm your potential client with too much information. You don't want them dropping off the page and going to your social media sites instead. You want your site to work as a simple transactional site where potential clients come and buy. Design a site so simple that even a non-techie can do it! All you do is sign up, plug in your information and click to buy. If this type of site does not suit your business think about a training program you can sell in relation to the use of the products you sell; a 4-week training program that can be sold as an automated PDF package that is self-service oriented. Create a trail period where your potential clients can try the product and if they like it can sign up after. *Focus@Will*, a neuroscience based music service that helps you focus, reduce distractions and retain information when working or studying do this with perfection. They offer a 15-day trial on their product. If you like it you are already signed up and just pay for the year to continue. It's a real online example of putting 'the brand in the hand'.

What to Do

When your potential client arrives at your sparklingly new website, guide them through a sales funnel. Everything they do should guide them closer to a purchase. On the home page give a choice to purchase A, B or C. When they click through, explain the offering in bullet points that leads them to the 'buy now' button. If you don't have this on your webpage, more than likely you have a brochure site with the standard home, about, products and contact buttons. On a sales focus site, there should be 2 functions:

- Buy now
- Learn more

'Buy now' is a straightforward call to action that leads to a transactional function. 'Learn more' is a button should build the relationship by answering questions from the potential client.

These questions may cover the old style about, why, product detail, and contact. Your objective here is to build the relationship and trust. Be sure that the 'learn more' always ends with the 'buy now' button.

Tips and Take Homes

As with any sales site, collect details so you can build your database with people who are interested in your product. Always give choices when selling. For example: the basic package, the light package, the lovely package and the high-end package. You can, of course, call these different things and appeal to different sensibilities.

Digital Nugget

Create a distinct domain name for your sales page. Create different product offerings. Design a tidy, concise explanatory page to cover your general business and information. The citybin.com is the domain name for The City Bin Co.'s main website. When the companyrun adverts, product launches and targeted campaigns they use www.citybin.ie This allows a focus and targeted message to reach the audience.

42. GO VIRAL

How it Works

Viral marketing is a tactic by which you create a marketing campaign with a deliberate aim of causing a quick and spontaneous spread of your message. Although viral marketing came into its full potential as a digital tool, its roots in marketing were well established before the birth of YouTube. Vinny Warren, a Galway born man based in Chicago Illinois, is noted in the marketing world as the creative genus behind the iconic *'Whassup?'* campaign for Budweiser that went viral. It became a household hit. The advert created an amusing way for the youth of the world to greet in person or by phone during the ad's 4-year campaign, which started in 1999. Viral has since become a more accessible reality with the growth of online marketing and video sharing platforms. The Dollar Shave Club's *Our Blades Are F**king Great* video is a textbook example of going viral. Within 48 hours of the video going live, the company had over 12,000 customers signed up for their services online. Using clever wit over brand supremacy to tell their story, they hooked a mass volume of potential customers through an engaging and well-scripted video. Michael Dubin, the video's star and company CEO spent $4,500 on the video and a minimum spent on Google ads.

What to Do

Video is your strongest message vehicle to access the biggest audience in the speediest manner that defines viral. Don't just make one video and tell yourself it doesn't work. To get the right script to work you must rework the content. Keep it snappy and short. Do something different and risque. Don't be afraid to poke fun at yourself or your brand. Look to create a strong emotional connection. Don't sell the brand, sell the story. The brand comes second. Hook them from the start. The shareability of the content is key to your viral success. Start with the unexpected. If people wouldn't expect you to have a gorilla in your videos that's exactly what you should put in your videos. What's your message? How can you tell it out of context while still getting the message across? Fill it with some silly fun!

Tips and Take Homes

Use traditional media to promote your online video. As it's hitting targets, send out press releases and screenshots with interesting backline stories and facts on the making of the viral video.

Digital Nugget

Sharing is what viral marketing is all about. Make sharing as easy as possible by allowing it to be shared, downloaded, embedded and commented on. Push it out by promoting it first. Fingers crossed for the snowball effect, but it's only going to happen if you tap into the emotional triggers that get people smiling and laughing. Think kids and cats! A viral video is a video first, made viral by viewers. It's not a viral video because you call it a viral video. Don't call it a viral video unless it actually is!

43. BUILD A GREAT WEBSITE

By Guest Author Ann Halloran

How it Works

There are a few different fundamentals to your website that you will need to consider. The basic 3 elements are:

1. **Domain Name** - This is the title of your website. It used to be important to have a strong related keyword in the title in order to get ranked - for example, something like *www.marketingtips.com* Current trends are to have shorter brand names (such as twitter, trello and so on). If you can fit in a related keyword in less than 10 characters, then go ahead and use it, but it is no longer essential. You can buy multiple domain names and redirect them to the website, for example: www.offlinemarketing.com. This can increase your chances of being found in searches.

2. **Web Hosting** - This is the space you book online to host your website files. Typically, you pay a monthly or annual subscription. The cost can depend on the level of activity you are expecting on your site.

3. **Content Management System (CMS)** - Your website consists of a set of files made up of code. Your web pages are typically saved in individual HTML (Hyper Text Markup Language) files. There will also be a CSS (Cascading Style Sheet) file which governs the look and feel of the website. Luckily, you don't need to learn code - CMSs are designed to make things easier for the end users - so all you will need to do is add your content and images in the spaces provided.

What to Do

Find a suitable domain name – Dotcom is good for reaching a worldwide audience. You can buy domain names from hosting companies, along with your hosting package. Look for a company that provides good customer care and a 24-hour service.

A popular CMS is wordpress.org. From this site, you can download files to create a website for free. You can also buy a theme that has styling and other features built in. Make sure that you choose a responsive design - so the website will automatically adjust to look good on mobile devices.

Tips and Take Homes

Before building your website, planning and research are essential. Who is your ideal customer? What problem do you solve for them? What makes you unique? How will you reach them? Build your content using search terms that are in demand. There are SEO tools available to help you find them. You only need to focus on one search term (keyword) per page or post. This will help you get ranked above your competition. Make sure that you have a strong internal linking system between pages on your site - so your visitors and the search engines don't get confused. The above steps will help you get your website ranking in the search engines *organically.* You can also spend money on advertising campaigns e,g, through Google or Facebook to get your website ranking high. Target and measure results of your advertising spend carefully for maximum return. For example, create adverts that direct visitors to a sales page rather than to your home page. Add Google Analytics code to your website so you can see what approaches are working for you, and what aren't.

Digital Nugget

Building an online business takes planning, patience and persistence – so stick with it and gave it time. Be active on social media and direct traffic to your website. Get others talking about you and your business. Having links to your site from authoritative sites as it will help raise your ranking.

44. USE E-COMMERCE TO SELL ONLINE

By Guest Author Darragh Canning

How it Works

Selling online and selling in-store has some similarities; you have products, you have customers and you take payments. That's where the affinity ends. Selling online is not like selling from a physical store. There is no human element, no salesperson, no physical product to pick up and examine. There is no friendly cashier to smile and wish you a good day! This means you have to think differently about your sales approach online.

What to Do

You're going to need an e-commerce platform! Once you know who your target market is, where they hang out online and what other sites they use, you can go about choosing an e-commerce platform. An e-commerce platform is the software that is used to manage the sale of products online.

If you're only selling 1-5 products then Paypal can be a great choice. It's quick to set up and can be easily linked to your bank account. Integrating Paypal into an existing website is also very straightforward. You can create 'Buy Now' buttons from your paypal dashboard and they will generate the code for you that means you can get your online shop up and running and start taking payments in no time! Selling 5-20 products? There is a package for you! Shopify is an amazingly simple service to set up, even for non-techies. Shopify is a 'hosted' solution, meaning they will take care of your hosting and bandwidth, ensuring that your site is always accessible to your customers. They even take daily backups just in case the unthinkable happens! 20 plus products? If you're feeling brave enough to manage your own 'self-hosted' solution there is no shortage of options out there. OpenCart, Magento, Zen Cart, WooCommerce and osCommerce are just a few that are available. These are dedicated ecommerce platforms built to handle large amounts of inventory and transactions. Each of these products do a wonderful job and it's just a matter of finding one that suits your needs. Although managing your own site and being in control of your files can be very rewarding it does require a certain level of technical competence.

Tips and Take Homes

Something that I see quite often is an e-commerce store using the manufacturers' description for their product pages. These descriptions are normally sent to every reseller of the product and is subsequently used by all of them; thus creating duplicate content. It is always best to create unique content or you could end up being pushed down the rankings.

Digital Nugget

Learn from the best! Sites like Amazon and Etsy are massively popular for a reason. Over the years they have analysed how their customers use their sites and used this information to improve sales and the user experience. Take note of what they do well. Apply these concepts to your site.

45. USE WEB ANALYTICS
TO GROW YOUR BUSINESS

By Guest Author Peter O'Neill

How it Works

Everyone working with websites should have heard of web analytics most likely through common tool – *Google Analytics*. It is so simple to use. Add one little bit of code to all pages on your website and it is job done! You will have lots of lovely reports to diligently read.

Key Lesson: Web analytics is not about reports, not even about data. *The purpose of Web Analytics is to provide intelligence that informs business actions leading to an improvement in performance.* If you are not using the data to make decisions, you may as well delete the code.

At their core, all Web Analytics tools are really simple (yes, there is more than Google Analytics! Some are free, while others are paid services). But they are all just tools. Like any tool, it needs to be the right tool for the job at hand. You have to know how to use it. In all cases, it simply requires that you add a snippet of code to all pages of your website. These days, you can manage this with a *Tag Management Solution* (Google offers a free tool here as well). The basic code does a lot of the work for you but then needs to be customised to capture all the really useful information. All campaign links that you use need to include URL query parameters that identify the campaign. Some tools can manage this automatically for you. The web analytics code can be customised to record more information about each page being viewed, information about the visitors to your website, capture details of their interactions with your website and record everything about purchases they make.

What to Do

There are 3 key steps required to get value from any web analytics tool:

1. Define what you need to know Hopefully, you already have your business objectives and a set of KPIs. What information do you need to measure your performance against these KPIs? What other business questions do you need to be able to answer? What actions and decisions are made in your business that could be smarter with the right information?

Get all this down on paper first so you know what you need from your web analytics tool.

3. Collect this information While a web analytics tool can provide a suite of reports out of the box, to get real value from the tool that enables you to answer your questions, you need to customise the tool. This requires you to invest resources into adding the right tagging to your website and configuring the tool itself.

4. **Be able to access the information** Now that you are collecting all this really valuable information, it is no good to you if you can't get your hands on it in a timely manner. Create easy to digest automated performance reporting. Ensure team members have the necessary training to know how to use the web analytics tool and how to interpret the numbers they are seeing.

All of this is enough to just get you started. The next step is to use the insights from the tool to make decisions and take actions.

Tips and Take Homes

There are so many things that you can do with web analytics. Here are a few ways in which web analytics can be used to improve business performance. Review the percentage of visitors seeing a 404 error page and identify the cause by recording the full URL of these pages. Record the number of search results. Create solutions for when popular terms have zero results. Record the form name, field name and error message for any form validation errors – add help pages or fix unnecessary validation issues. Review funnel performance by visitor type, device type, browser, traffic source, country, entry point and anything else you can think of. Look for funnel stages in segments which underperform, find out why and fix the problems. If a retailer, review product performance based on their add to basket rate (Add to basket/sessions viewed) and not just sales. Underperforming products could be due to poor availability, bad images, bad copy, bad reviews or too high a price. Look for products with high 'add to Basket' rate but low views, promote these every way you can. If you are a publisher, use the same approach when evaluating the best/worst content pieces on your website. Use the read rate or share rate. Beyond all this though, there are two key pieces of advice to give anyone looking at web analytics. The first is to take small steps, start simple and build from there. The second is to take advantage of the large quantity of resources that are available online to learn about web analytics and to answer any questions you have.

Digital Nugget

Web analytics is about working smarter. The tools are incredibly powerful and can deliver massive rewards for your business. That means they can be very complicated and may need a small investment of resources to get at the insights and real value. To add the basic tag to all pages is really quick and easy. To set up the tool properly takes time and expertise. To change the way a business thinks and operates is really difficult and takes a long time. But the potential payoff for doing so, for converting a business to making decisions based on data, is absolutely massive.

46. USE FACEBOOK
TO GROW YOUR BUSINESS

By Guest Author Jenny Brennan

How it Works:

As a social media channel, *Facebook* can be a love or hate relationship for small business owners (SME's). The main reason for this is that Facebook has been so transparent in the data it has given us. We tend to measure our success on Facebook based on how many people we reach. This is just a vanity metric. As a small business, this is the wrong metric to focus on. Businesses need to start using the network as a way to increase their visibility with their ideal market. They need to position themselves as an expert. They have to build a sales funnel that drives fans to valuable content that converts to more business.

Before we look at the way it works, we need to understand that Facebook is an ever-changing platform. If you view Facebook as a free platform to broadcast your marketing messages, focus on the vanity metrics and expect it to transform your business this way. It's time to look for another way to sell your products and services. Facebook can be used as an effective sales funnel. Below I have highlighted 4 essential steps to focus on as outlined by Jon Loomer.

1. Attract relevant fans
2. Provide value
3. Collect e-mail addresses
4. Sell

Each of these steps may vary for your business, but the theory and journey that you bring your fans on should be similar and consistent. The opportunities on Facebook for business are vast.

The adverts platform alone lets us target website visitors, visitors who have abandoned shopping carts, our customers, our fans, people who look like our fans, website traffic and customers and people who are interested in our competition.

What to Do

There is value in using Facebook when done right. You need to be strategic in how you are going to reach your goals and what resources you need to do this.

1. Set Goals

Tony Robbins once said, *"Setting goals is the first step to turning the invisible into the visible."*

The number of businesses who fail to make and write down Facebook marketing goals still surprises me.

If you want to know how you are performing and what is working, setting goals is the first step to your long-term success. Below I have outlined an example of goals that you can use as a guide:

- Increase quality fans by x% every month (These should be based on custom audiences)
- Increase web traffic by x% per month
- Increase leads by x per month
- Increase direct inquiries by X per month
- Increase online bookings by X%
- Increase footfall by X per month
- Fill events with X people

Your goals are going to vary depending on what you want to achieve. Note that all of the above are measurable.

2. Plan

To reach your goals you are going to need a plan to get there. Here are some of the essential elements you are going to include in that plan.

- Marketing budget
- Outline goals
- Design and page set-up
- Resources - admins
- Website - landing pages – e-mail marketing
- Content plan - both native posts for Facebook, your own blog content and third party content

- Visual and video content plan
- Daily posting schedule
- Contests
- Facebook marketing tools
- Facebook adverts
- Timelines

These tools are a plus for your Facebook marketing efforts. If you have a small budget there are a number of free options available.

Useful Facebook Tools:

- Agorapulse
- Ads Espresso
- Ads Roll
- Buffer
- Canva
- Conversation score
- Edgerank checker
- Fan Page Karma
- Heyo
- Likealyser
- Shortstack
- Tabsite
- Postplanner

Use tools like *Canva* to create visually appealing Facebook posts.
Use *Facebook's Pages Manager App* to manage your page via mobile.

Tips and Take Homes

There are many tips that I could share to help you, but here are the ones that I have tried and tested for both my business and that of my clients:

1. **Provide value:** Use Facebook to provide your fans, readers and prospects with valuable content that will help, entertain or educate them.

2. **Build your list with Facebook:** 91 percent of consumers check email every day. I would recommend you create a highly valuable lead magnet that will help you attract relevant subscribers.

3. **Be consistent:** Make sure that you have a content calendar and a posting strategy. Consistency is a long term but essential strategy to building trust with fans.

4. **Include your fans:** Ask your fans regularly what they want. This will help you to decide what exclusive offers to create, the type of content you need and proves that you genuinely care about your fans.

5. **Use video:** One of the biggest trends on Facebook is video. Share product infomation, tips, and interviews. Use video to help your fans connect with you on another level.

6. **Invest in adverts:** Would you pay a local paper or radio to advertise your business? You need to start viewing Facebook in the same light. The great benefit of Facebook ads is that you can measure what works and what doesn't. Even if you have a small €1 daily budget, you can reach more people.

Digital Nugget

Brands can use Facebook to broadcast their marketing messages and focus on metrics such as likes, clicks and reach. These brands are only leveraging a small part of what is possible with Facebook. Businesses who are really experiencing the benefits of Facebook are those who are using it to build a relationship with people who have a need for helpful, entertaining and valuable content. As a result, this brings the fans on a journey that improves visibility and builds trust, which leads to more sales.

47. GROW YOUR BUSINESS ON TWITTER

By Guest Author Samantha Kelly

How it Works:

Twitter is a social network that shares 140 character (max) messages called *Tweets*. You follow people and people follow you. You share information, pictures, opinions and videos. That means that you can make a statement or sentence and put it out there to whoever is following you. Make your profile look so interesting that people will want to click on you. Your followers are also your very own marketing team. They are the ones who will decide if you are interesting enough or if your content (what you say in your tweets) is good enough to retweet to their followers. They are the ones who will share your tweets and help you to trend.

What to Do

Let's start at the begining! If you are a small business owner I recommend you use your picture. This attracts people and makes you look more personable. You can put your logo or icon on the header section of your profile. If you are a large company use your company logo. A hotel? A picture of the hotel. Keep your *bio* short and interesting. Tell people who you are, what you do and your likes (e.g. hobbies, etc.) You want to attract like-minded individual. People buy from people so even if you are a company make it sound like you are approachable and that you are going to be tweeting interesting tweets. Or, even better, be yourself! Think of the buyer persona of your clients. What do they want to talk or read about? What pictures or videos would they be in to? There is section to edit your profile so you put your website link into your bio so that when people look at your profile they can simply 'click' to go straight to your website! Click on the 'profile' settings section to edit your profile. If your a newbie, write your first tweet! Start by saying something like.... *'Hi Everyone, I am new to twitter! #Newbie'* - Keep it simple and be yourself. Then continue to search for people to follow. For example, if you like gardening or sell garden plants and tools, search for any tweets that mentions #gardening in the search box. Twitter will also suggest others to follow. You can refresh these suggestions if you want to search for more. Look at what the people you follow are saying. Get involved and click *reply* if you want to add to the conversation! Click *retweet* if you want to share their tweet with your own followers. Click on the *notification* button to see who has mentioned you. If you click on *home*, this will bring you to your Twitter feed. These are the tweets of everyone you are following! If you want to tweet someone you follow simply click on the tweet button and put their Twitter name into the tweet. This is the *compose* tweet button. You can tweet away and connect with your audience.

Tips and Take Homes

If your target market is 35-55 year olds, professional and urban, then Twitter is worth putting some time into. If your target market is teens you may need to look into *Instagram* or *Snapchat.* Not every platform will work for your business. Twitter has so much power that when used wisely it can really help you get those sales you need and create a buzz around your brand. Here are some tips to get your Twitter account working for you:

1. Make sure your bio is interesting. Does it say exactly what you do? Why should I follow you? Tell me something about your business or yourself. What do you do? What do you sell? What kind of things will you be tweeting about?

2. Connect with like-minded people. Start following people who tweet about business if you are interested in business topics. If you are in the craft business, follow similar accounts or others who run events or tweet about crafting. Start following Twitter accounts that you would be interested in yourself and that have a connection to your business and your customers! No point in following accounts that aren't going to help you grow on Twitter!

3. Tweet often. I recommend doing 10 Tweets per day. 3 of these can be sales type tweets directing people to a 'buy now' or 'book now' page. But most of your tweets should be either interesting content or pictures related to you or your industry in a fun, lighthearted and sharable way. Show your followers that you have interesting stuff to say. Show that you know your stuff and you are the expert in what you do.

4. If you are stuck for time, hit the peak times on Twitter. The morning commute, break-times and lunchtime are busy times on Twitter. If you are a restaurant owner, tweet just before lunch, with a tasty looking picture of a meal! You never know, someone might be in your area at that time feeling a little peckish and you will

make the decision for them about where they are heading to eat! Another peek time is 9-11pm at night.

5. Get involved in Tweet chats! There are many chats on Twitter. Find one related to your business or even just one you like yourself. Some great hashtags to get involved in are:

- #Irishbizparty - For SMEs - from 9-11pm
  Every Wednesday @irishbizparty
- #Britishbizparty - For UK business owners - from 9-10pm
  Every Monday @Britishbizparty
- #Belfasthour - For SMEs in Northern Ireland
  Every Thursday from 9-10pm @BelfasthourNI

Digital Nugget

Tweet at busy times. The busiest times on Twitter are: 7-9am - Morning commute 10-11am - Coffee break 1-3pm - Lunchtime 5-7pm - Evening commute 9-11pm - Kids have gone to bed and lots of prime time TV programs are on the television. The main thing to remember is: Be active and support others with retweets. Use relevant and interesting content and use pictures where possible. Be positive and keep away from controversy. Grow your business by being yourself!

BUILD A SUPER-SOLID BUSINESS BRAND

All the big brands started somewhere small. They grew into known household names over time with huge commitment and learning from their failures. When they fell down they got up again. When something didn't work, they tried something different. They never stopped. You have so many case studies of great brands to turn to and research the methods they applied; however, in the end I believe you will take a little from the success of others and apply your own wisdom.

Your brand is much more than your name or your logo. It's the culture. It's the consistency. It's the trust and confidence that the buying public is willing to put into you based on their experiences. It's a type of language that gives a sense of identity to your brand. It's a growing personality that customers can connect with and relate to. A great brand is coherent and strong. The best way to do this is to create brand guidelines around the logo, the culture, the people and the customers.

Define your brand. Learn its strengths and use them. Look for the weaknesses and improve them. Place your brand where your potential customer will see it. Place it in their hand. Shine a light on the brand colours. Amplify them. Raise the standard of your brand and how people see it by winning awards and associating your brand with awards. Create a catchy tagline true to your brand that customers will remember.

Look good. Let an appearance or uniform communicate your message. It will let people know where you are. It will add a sense of professionalism. It makes you easily identifiable. It's not always about fitting in. To be seen you have to make an effort to stand out.

Talk to your top customers. Give them an opportunity to become your top promotors and brand ambassadors. Make brand promises that will set the standards. Promote a great service and delivery of your product.

Start up to scale up! If you are going to grow a brand start thinking big from day one. Think about how your brand colours, logo and culture will look, feel and translate into different parts of the world. Most importantly, be true to yourself and your brand values.

48. SHOUT YOUR BRAND NAME FROM THE ROOFTOPS

How it Works

In the summer of 2014 I was flying home to Ireland on a Ryanair flight from sunny Valencia in Spain. As we were approaching Dublin airport, I saw one of the best and simplest marketing tools I've ever seen. I was amazed. One building stood out to me as the plane flew over the buildings into Dublin airport. It had *bewleys.com* printed along the length of its roof in big bold letters. You couldn't miss it (if you were on the plane!) I didn't go off and buy myself a big trolley of Bewley's products; however, their brand stood out. It became so imprinted in my mind that a few days later when I was doing the weekly shopping I couldn't but help take note when I was passing the Bewley's range of teas and coffees. This is the power of the subconscious mind!

Rooftop marketing was a new concept for me. From that day on I have seen numerous examples. In fact, I saw a similar example two days later when collecting my Volkswagen T5 high roof campervan that I was getting upgraded with a new interior & body re-spray. Paul Devane of *Autolux* who was doing the work for me brought me up to the second level of his workshop to look down at the roof of van. He thought I'd be a bit unhappy over what I was about to see. Written across the surface of the top of the van was *DSM, Data Storage & Management Ltd, The Professional Records Management Company*. I laughed. Far from being annoyed, I was delighted. Paul showed me another example of a company using its roof to advertise to its target market. A business that knew it had to reach offices situated above the first floor looking out on to the street.

What to Do

Shout your brand name or web address from the rooftops. If you don't have a building that is geographically placed to catch overhead flying traffic or a fleet of vans that can be branded on their rooftop, ask yourself who does. There is an opportunity for branding partnership and for creating publicity in the media from the unusual branding of a building, rooftop or vehicle. Imagine when people go to click on the aerial view of a group on buildings on Google Earth and in amongst the clutter of buildings and busy streets they see your logo on a building roof or on top of a commercial vehicle.

Tips and Take Homes

If rooftop marketing is for your business do it. If you have a roof and don't see a value or opportunity in using it for your own brand, let others use it. You can always monetise it by renting the space to others who can post their promotional messages on top of your building or on the rooftop of your fleet of cars, vans and trucks. Businesses always advertise on the side and front of buildings, cars and vans, but rarely on top!

Digital Nugget

Post photos of your bird's eye view branding to the different online photography platforms. Blog about the unusual advertising method you used and why you did it. Write up a press release drawing attention to your curious use of space and send it out to the local media.

49. PLACE A FACE ON YOUR BRAND AND WATCH YOUR SALES GROW

How it Works

People connect with people. In business you need to show that you aren't just some nameless team hiding behind a logo. The best brands are personable, contactable and human. When we think of Richard Branson we automatically connect his name to Virgin. He is the face and voice of his brand. Supervalu, a successful chain of Irish supermarkets, has a picture of the individual store managers on pop up banners and overhead signs welcoming customers to each one of their stores. I know when I walk into my local Supervalu in the village of Oranmore, Galway in the west of Ireland that Liam Coady is the store manager. Liam is on the floor talking to customers, helping customers and building strong customer relationships. His face seems familiar. That's because his photo appears on posters and leaflets. This is why I and countless other loyal clients come back time after time. There are 3 other well known big branded supermarkets in the same area but none of them are doing it like Supervalu.

From the CEO of the company to the person on the frontline delivering the service, a face adds personality, friendliness and trust to your brand. This is what Richard Branson and every Supervalu manager does well and what you can start doing for your business today. People know brands and identify with people and their story. The equation is simple: One friendly face plus one strong brand equals powerful relationship marketing. Make a commitment to add your smile to promotional material and reap the benefits of familiarity and personality with customer loyalty.

What to Do

If you are in a service industry or involved in the sales of a product which has first hand contact with people, it's important to have a friendly recognisable face so that potential clients can feel that there is already a relationship. When a decision to purchase your offering is made there is a predicted sense of familiarity. This strengthens relationships and rapport for future sales. Hire a professional photographer to take some profile and full-length photos of you or the person who will be the face of the company. Use these images consistently with your brand. Make sure the same face always appears on all media adverts from your online adverts to the local newspapers.

Tips and Take Homes

Put a face to your brand and watch your sales grow. In doing so, you create new content which strengthens marketing efforts online and offline by having your face on the website, video presentations, products, leaflets, outdoor billboards and all other traditional media advertising. Use your image or that of the person who will represent your brand to tell the business story. Think of all the places that potential clients will see your brand. Ask if there is a case for putting a friendly image of you to support the sale.

Digital Nugget

Start with recording a welcome video with you or the 'top dog' in the company. Introduce yourself as the face of your company. Make a short video of your workforce saying a quick hello and introducing themselves to post on your website and social media channels. This will show your business and its friendly personality.

50. SELL YOUR BRAND COLOUR

How it Works

Colour psychology is not something you hear too often in the business world, yet the creative amongst us fly the flag for the power of colour and the effect it may have on customer engagement. Naturally, as business owners, you want to attract new customers and not deter them, so it's really important to look at small details such as the colour used in your business logos, shop fronts, interior settings, and the products themselves. Are the colours attractive? Do the colours enhance your business and your brand? A shop front painted black on a dark side street might not look very tempting on a rainy day. So, if your business was a colour, which colour would it be? Red, blue, orange, black? Would it be loud, soft or subtle?

I love it when the local newspaper, the Galway Advertiser comes through our letterbox every Thursday. The one thing that catches my eye every week is the colour of the logo. It's Red. When The City Bin Co.'s bins are out for collection you will know about it because all you will see is a sea of red bins. It is consistent and delivered with one of the strongest colours on the artist's palette. Red is powerful, eye catching and enthusiastic. Red is a primary colour that gets noticed with very warm, exciting, and strong virtues. You only have to look at companies such as Virgin and Cola-Cola to see the value of red. Now, let's not give all the glory to the red brands as many other colours carry different strengths and meaning. Green is an earth colour that is associated with healing, growth and harmony. Green is also related to the environment and sustainable business practices. Examples of Green brands are Starbucks coffee and Heineken, and of course, green is a great colour for brand Ireland. Blue is seen as reliable, dependable, and dedicated. Averda, the largest environmental solutions provider in the MENA region is blue. The pharmacy chain Boots is blue. The Middle Eastern business Cobone.com, which was founded by Irish entrepreneur Paul Kenny is blue. The one thing that all these brands have in common is that they put a lot of thought into developing and creating a brand that could grow. Colour plays a big part in the creative process.

The colour you use in your branding can give personality to your business. It can attract your customer's eye. The right colour can get you noticed and make your business and brand instantly recognizable. It can allow you to stand out from your competitors.

What to Do

If your business is already established and you feel the logo or brand colour is weak, you can still change things. Some of the best-known brands in the world have redesigned their look and logo, such as Apple, Starbucks and Electric Ireland. Review your existing brand and the current colours and design. Does it reflect your brand's authentic values? Make sure your brand is instantly recognisable in such a way that customers can immediately identify with a certain desire to explore what you have to offer through the branding. Keep your brand simple and easy to know. When you take time to reflect and assess the design, colour, logo, and overall appearance of your business, you give yourself a huge opportunity to improve, redesign, rebrand and re-launch your business. Ask yourself: what's the colour of your business and does it express a personality or a mood? Is it strong? Is it happy? Is it welcoming? Is it impressive and easy to remember? Is it time to rebrand and re-launch?

Tips and Take Homes

Colour is an asset for any company who uses it right from having instantly recognisable products to re-marketing your brand to new potential clients. This creates a new awareness and re-engages with existing customers. Talk to a designer about your needs and take on board their professional opinion.

Digital Nugget

Make sure the colour on your website, social media and online adverts is consistent with the colour used in your offline material. When you go to your printer or designer for marketing material such as booklets or business cards, be sure to show them the colours you use on your online logos and banners. No point in having red text in one place and pink in the next. The customer may not recognise the brand!

51. BE AN AWARD WINNING COMPANY

How it Works

The City Bin Co. has repeatedly entered and won many awards since the company started. They won the *Deloitte Best Managed Companies' Award* 4 times in a row, 2009 – 2012 and the *European Business Awards' National Champions in Customer Service 2013*. The company has an award winning mindset and the strength and confidence to be gained from this is immeasurable. The benefits from a PR, marketing and networking point of view are invaluable.

Participating in an award can create new opportunities from PR exposure, create brand awareness, open doors for your product and allow you to network with potential costumers and partners. It can improve employee morale. It can influence both existing and potential customers.

Calling yourself an 'awarding winning company' helps potential customers to better understand your offerings and it sends out positive indications to browsing eyes that you are a winner. Such an exercise doesn't just oblige you to do a laser focus examination of your company; it compels you to 'up your game.' You create new benchmarks that make you and your team go for gold and get better results. You look deeply at the competitors and other businesses competing for the award to figure out the points of difference. To win or grab PR attention, the company will have to tighten up the operational element on all levels. You will have to take a really hard honest look under the hood before you enter. There are lots of oil and pit-stop checks as you go through the process. This is often worth more than the award itself.

What to Do

Make the decision to enter awards and commit to it. Make it company policy. Firstly look at your strengths. Are you strong in marketing, sales, customer service, online, retail or any niche area that defines your company? These are the awards you should be looking to be associated with. Look locally, nationally and globally for such awards. Look at the websites for local councils, networking groups, chambers of commerce, business schools and conferences. If you can't find them, read the next chapter!

There are two initial reasons to enter awards 1) the prize and 2) the publicity. When you find an award you would like to enter, it's normally a straightforward application process. You can be nominated or more usually you nominate yourself! In this process you might fill out a brief application outlining background, timeline, achievements and forecasts. Often these awards involve interviews with a panel of judges who will be part of the process in shortlisting the finalists and an awards presentation event. At every point, document your progress and achievement by blogging and issuing press releases to the local papers of your successes throughout the awards. In many cases this adds up to free marketing for your business that improves brand awareness. Maybe free is too cheap a word? You pay with hard work and strong team management and focused goals.

When I spoke to Adrian Tripp, CEO of the European Business Awards, he said, *"The key elements that the champions and winners of the European Businesses Awards display are innovation, growth, strategic thinking, a focus on customers, investment in people, giving back to the communities, the economy and the environment."*

Tips and Take Homes

Don't accept time and resources constraints as excuses not to pursue awards. Make it happen. The positives for entering outweigh the excuses for not doing so. If you become a nominee, finalist or overall winner, be sure to place this information on company docket books, receipts, adverts, blogs, websites, and invoices. Mention it on all possible communication channels to your clients. Reinforce the value of your brand and the offering with the awards that you have won. Don't just enter once. Keep doing it. Make it the norm. Just because you don't make it this year doesn't mean you won't be there the following year. Look at business awards as a benchmark and company goal setters. Look at the marketing material before, during and after the event. Research the past winners. Connect with them and speak to them about their experience. The fact that you participate is a real seal of quality for potential customers. And if you win, that's the icing on the cake. You can then call yourself an award winning company!

Digital Nugget

When you go for an award use your social media channels to communicate your progress. Don't just tell customers when you have won. Tell them the reason why you have entered and keep them updated along the way.

52. ASSOCIATE YOUR BRAND WITH AWARDS

How it Works

If you can't find awards or competitions for your business to enter and win that benefit you professionally or if you are getting bored winning awards, why not start an award and put your company's name and brand behind it? It could be to acknowledge top performers in your industry. It could be an award that is related to your customers or it could be totally unrelated and supportive of a certain collective. Imagine the 'Your Business Name' 'Something' people of the year awards. In many ways it doesn't really matter what that something is as long as you back it. This is a great way to grow brand awareness. It allows you to place your logo on front of people who would not normally be familiar with your brand. When I was in my early 20's, I had aspirations to be a professional songwriter and entered the *Hotpress/Bacardi* song of the year. I was one of the finalists. Yes, it's a big jump from the music business to the waste industry where we won the *Deloitte Best Managed Companies' Award*, but in both cases there was a lot of press coverage all of which mentioned the brand sponsoring the awards as much as the winners.

I'm also a big fan of the *Bord Gáis Energy Irish book Awards* and with a bit of luck I will win someday in the future! The point here is that the awards don't have the same appeal without the support of the named identity or awards sponsor. By linking your brand with awards you create an association with a wider audience. This gives you the opportunity to be linked to that created space year in and year out. You create a networking funnel where you can promote your brand and products. You create a goodwill identity where all people involved gain added publicity through their own marketing channels promoting their participation in their award. The Deloitte brand is on the bottom of The City Bin Co.'s headed paper and on our website. Their brand has become a badge of honour. This is possible to do at any level: local, national or international. You will get out of it what you put in.

In 2013, along with the founder of *Online Marketing in Galway* Maricka Burke Keogh, I conceived the idea for the 1st OMiG Awards. The *Connaught Tribune* and *the Galway City Enterprise Board* sponsored the event. The event took place within 6 months of the idea being brainstormed over a spaghetti bolognese with Maricka.

There were over 250 business people in attendance, 5 Awards for the best marketers in the West of Ireland, and a prize to the value of 25,000 euros. The awards ceremony was repeated the following year and and has become an annual highlight in the local business calendar.

What to Do

Ask yourself what is missing in your region. What has a large community but no recognition? Focus on one theme. It may be something in your industry, in the arts, in fashion or in your community. You need to design the awards ceremony and work backwards. How many awards? What will be the categories? Where will it be? Will there be a prize or are the awards by name sufficient? What will be the application process? And how will you market it? From the word 'go' you need to put a team together to manage the different elements of the event. Set a deadline with a plan of action timeframe and stick to it. Keep the branding consistent. Start small for the first year and grow it year on year. This enables you to understand what works and what doesn't work. You can apply a new strategy each time that will benefit and enhance the awards. Hire a professional photographer to take pictures during the ceremony and then afterwards with each award recipient and key sponsors. Use these photographs for your press release, tradition media and your social media platforms.

Tips and Take Homes

Create an award ceremony that will benefit others and will be remembered. Make this an event that people will not want to miss. When Patrick McDermott, Managing Director of Stocktaking.ie won the JCI Galway entrepreneur of the year in 2013 he said: *"The amazing thing that comes with the winning of the award is not just the prize, publicity and marketing but the credibility it brings to the business."* The JCI brand is on their website, yet another badge of honour pinned up with pride. Keep the process and final ceremony fun, short and snappy. The fewer categories created for the awards the better the value of the awards. The Sales Master Master's Awards have only one award each year: 'Sales Person of the Year Award.' This exclusivity gives greater importance to the award.

Digital Nugget

Be sure you create a badge for nominees, finalists and winners that can be linked back to your website and placed on all the participants' websites.

53. CREATE A CATCHY CORPORATE TAGLINE

How it Works

When Gerry Duffy, professional speaker and writer on motivation and goal setting spoke at a Sales Master Masters event in July 2014 everybody stood up and did their quick one-line introduction. At the end of the talk Gerry pointed out the importance of being unique and different and catching people's attention. He said that one introduction stood out above the rest. That was when Robert Creane, who specialises in the treatment of back pain, stood up and said, *"Hi I'm Rob Creane from the Deerpark Clinic. We'll break our backs to fix yours".* He got an instant reaction from everybody in the room. It was catchy. It was different and it was creative. Without saying directly what he did, we all knew. Through one tagline on his business introduction he built instant rapport with everybody in the room. I was not surprised when I saw the same tagline repeated on his business card. It was different and simple. It spoke directly to his target audience, and carried the human touch with a pinch of good humour.

What to Do

If there is one phrase you want people to remember when they think of your brand what would it be? For McDonalds it is *'I'm loving it!* And for M&M's it's *'melts in your mouth and not in your hands.'* What results do you want to generate? What reaction do you want from the people listening to it?

Start by writing down a list of words or phrases that communicate a message that emotionally captures your potential customer. Do this to investigate how your current clients feel about your brand.

Get your current customers involved by inviting them to answer the following question? Describe our service or your experience with our product in one word, a phrase or a short sentence. You will be surprised at what you might receive and with a bit of luck you will get a small collection of short positive testimonials! Use the feedback to create a list to generate new ideas. Make a shortlist of your top 10 preferences. Within the chosen few, do a brainstorming session using wordplay, rhyming, alliterations and synonyms to find your catchy corporate tagline.

Tips and Take Homes

Keep it simple and to the point. It's always the simplest slogans that stick. Use humour to communicate your message. Test your tagline within a selection of your existing customer base. If it isn't getting a reaction, go back to the drawing board and rewrite until you get it right! When you get to the point where you are happy with your corporate tagline make sure you roll it out with consistency. Everywhere your logo is your corporate tagline can appear.

Digital Nugget

Create a click through where your corporate tagline appears on your website. Allow this to bring the user to a video or blog detailing the process of how you came up with the tagline, who was involved and why you say what you say. Bring the customers behind the scenes. Use it as an opportunity to explain more about why you do what you do. Let your tagline tell your story.

54. OUTLINE YOUR BRAND GUIDELINES

How it Works

A brand true to its name is confident and strong to the point that the brand name is enough for a purchase to be made. Apple and Virgin are great examples of really strong brands that motivate consumers to buy solely on love and trust of the brand over product. To implement successful brand guidelines, you have to create an identifiable brand for your business. You want potential customers to relate to you and all that your business represents. The consistency of images, colours, fonts and ratio of text to image all play an important role in brand development. The people working in the business, the customers, the product and the service all represent the brand and the overall feel and tone that eventually creates the reasons people buy your products. The important thing is a clear distinctiveness throughout your business. This is the brand. It's like an unmistakable personality. The best way to achieve it is to write it down in black and white. With the groundwork on paper, you can let it grow and develop.

What to Do

Create a set of design guidelines that bind the look and feel of all your marketing and promotional materials. These guidelines act as a standard benchmark for anybody involved in the use of the brand. This practice will better position you to create brand awareness and differentiate your brand from your competition. When designing a brand you have to think of the logo, but there are so many more elements at play. For example, you need to focus on the words associated with your brand. Give time to developing the company culture. The brand will be shaped by the culture of your company. The public perception of your products will play an immense part in determining the strength of your brand. You have full responsibility for both the culture and the product. Map out all the touch points where your customer comes into contact with the brand.

Begin by creating an action plan for your brand. Develop brand guidelines that state all information about the logo. This is useful to have when giving your logo to designers to produce promotional material. You want your logo to be placed in a certain position on every product, promotional material and premises. You want the logo to be exactly the same every time. Give attention to the tone of the text used across all products, websites and communications.

Make sure there is a thread in the language used. Hilary Foley, CEO of the international heath food company, Nua Natural, is a great example of this. Every product and every display unit shows her brand with impeccable results. From product to market it never changes. This creates instant recognition. Hilary does not deviate from her brand guidelines no matter how big the temptation. Familiarity is what brings her customers back again and again. When you veer from your logo design, message tone and brand feel, it is comparable to speaking a different language. A slight change in what might be considered irrelevant detail such as the font, the colour or the size means you are not branding, you are redesigning the trademark of your business.

Tips and Take Homes

Create a file with all relevant data in relation to your brand including logo, font, colour, positioning, associated words, and brand taglines. This can be used when getting third party collaborative work done on your business. Clear-cut guidelines create less room for disappointments.

Digital Nugget

When you are too strict on the brand guidelines it can kill creativity within the business. Use online tools such as blogging or photo hosting platforms to share the creativity with the brand and logo. After all, in contrast to keeping your brand the same at every possible viewing point, notice that Google change their logo daily on their search engine. They are certainly not losing brand familiarity and that, too, is an interesting strategy.

55. PUT YOUR BRAND IN THE HAND

How it Works

Familiarity sells. To gain familiarity, you need to put your brand into the hands of your potential client. Print your logo and call to action on tangible items. One place to start is to gift your existing clients with wearable and branded promotional gifts for their loyalty and commitment to your product. Existing customers don't need to be convinced of your value. This 'brand in the hand' marketing also reinforces the familiarity of the brand with those already converted. You can have people wearing your logo printed t-shirts breeding brand awareness on the streets before your products have had a chance to hit the shelves.

What to Do

Research the profile of your existing clients to see what they wear and where they hang out. Look at their demographic segmentation. For example, if they fall between the ages of 18 and 30, an affiliation with a music venue could do the trick. Look at cool clothing such as hoodies and hats. If they fall into the family bracket look at child safety. Maybe a few branded umbrellas could be in order if your clients come from a wet country such as Ireland. Look at pens for your clients to write their shopping list! The purpose of branding promotional material and wearable items is that your loyal followers become walking billboards for your brand. Everyday people can be seen enjoying their takeaway coffee. The paper cup is normally branded with the logo of the coffee or the business where the coffee was purchased. In some cases there is no logo on the cup. You could partner with the coffee house, pay the price of their cups in exchange for your brand on their product. Place your brand in the hand of young busy professionals as they enjoy their coffee!

Tips and Take Homes

This is the grey area in the marketing world. Lets face it, you can print a million pens and t-shirts tomorrow but they get lost in the endless piles of pens and t-shirts that companies hand out every day. I am certainly guilty of having a dozen branded freebies in my car. Within them there is only one that stands out. That is the Stocktaking.ie pen. It was hand delivered by the CEO of the company Patrick McDermott. Patrick knew that for the promotional material to be effective you must be personal and you must be different. One way to do this is in the delivery.

It's better to print up a minimum order of a promotional item and hand-deliver them to your top 100 clients than to spend big bucks on thousands of items and blindly post them to everybody. After all, sales is psychology.

Digital Nugget

Technology has made the phone the 'ultimate brand in the hand' item that all people interact with. Look inside and outside the new human attachment. Look at useful phone accessories that can incorporate your logo. Build a simple game app that displays your logo at the beginning. You never know you could be responsible for the next *Angry Birds*. Now, that would not be a bad thing!

56. GET SUITED AND BOOTED

How it Works

Get suited and booted with a branded uniform. This creates visibility. If you and your employees are wearing a uniform it promotes a feeling of unison and equality. This is good for employee self esteem and customer perception. A uniform will help your employees take ownership of your brand. They will feel part of a team. This can lead to an increase in productivity. Uniforms can say a lot about your standards. The best way to look professional and stand out from the crowd is by introducing branded uniforms. This will immediately improve visiblisibility. Every member of your uniformed team becomes a moving advertisement. And if it is only you on the payroll, well you too can wear a uniform!

Gene Browne, CEO of The City Bin Co., first introduced the idea of a branded uniform to the company after observing *UPS* drivers and their iconic brown uniform. When The City Bin Co. launched its uniform in 1998, a local paper, *The Sentinel*, wrote about '*the new look of the smart and well presented staff of The City Bin Co.*' - This wasn't the norm in waste collection and The City Bin Co. was the exception to the rule. The readily identifiable uniform reversed the perception of the tired, traditional bin man. The City Bin Co. uniform stood out from competitors and told the public that this person works for The City Bin Co. and is here to serve. The uniform consisted of red trousers, red polo shirt, a cool red 'soccer style' jacket and a red peaked cap, with each piece sporting high visibility strips. It was consistent with the brand colours and quality.

When the uniform was launched it had such an impact that stay at home mums started to blog about it saying that they felt James Bond had just collected their bins. One blog read: "*His overalls are so spanky clean, he might be wearing a tux....007 wheels the bin over to the truck.*".

RTE Radio One's Business Show subsequently picked up on the blog and had Gene Browne on in a 'tongue in cheek' piece to discuss the mums' reaction. Somebody in uniform projects an image of reliability, strength, safety and trust. – Again psychology. That is certainly the case when it comes to The City Bin Co.'s uniform. A uniform creates visibility and allows your brand to be distinctive and easily identifiable to the general public.

What to Do

Design your uniform to reflect your company's culture and values. Align your colours, logo and style with the overall branding style that represents your business. Investigate the existing uniforms within your industry and outside it also. Look at national and international styles. See what stands out. See what sings 'service' from a single glance. Think of where you or your employees will be positioned and the climate both indoors or outdoors. Have a winter and summer uniform. Have an official and casual version. When you have your uniform designed and ready to go make a big deal about it. You could blog about its creation from start to finish. Set out clear guidelines in relation to your company uniform. Describe it and state where it must be worn and where it must not be worn.

Tips and Take Homes

When designing the uniform ask your employees and customers for their input. These are the people that will be wearing and looking at your brand. It is a good team building exercise to get everybody involved from the start and really important as your staff are the front face of your business. If they wear the company with pride, this will resonate with your customers.

Digital Nugget

Create a merchandise line of some of your uniform such as t-shirts and hats. This promotional clothing could be sold in your online store. Wearable merchandise is a great way to generate brand visibility. Make sure it is different from the official uniform and of course, that it oozes coolness.

57. BRING ON THE BRAND AMBASSADORS

How it Works

Great marketing happens when you tap in to the community or create a community of customers who believe in what you do. When you find or create a community around your brand, you form the perfect environment to appoint brand ambassadors. These are people who use your product, promote your brand and love your brand so much they will recommend it to others.

What to Do

Launch a brand ambassador programme that converts your best customers into your best sales force. Make your selected ambassador feel as if they are part of the team. Bring them inside your company. Make them feel part of your brand. Have an annual brand ambassador event. Design brand ambassador uniforms or identity cards. Give your brand ambassadors sneak previews of your new products. Invite them to participate in the service design or product marketing design. Ask them to test your new products. Consider your brand ambassadors to be extended and treasured members of your core team.

Tips and Take Homes

Make brand ambassador involvement restricted. You don't want all your clients to be members of your brand ambassador program. It's better to have a team of 5 dedicated ambassadors working closely together and singing the same song. You don't want to have a high quantity of unmanageable ambassadors all going in different directions.

Digital Nugget

Invite your brand ambassadors to create excellent content for your blog and marketing campaigns. They could create video blogs, user stories, tips for starters and testimonials for you to use on your website and share them on your social media channels.

58. DEFINE YOUR BRAND

How it Works

A brilliant brand is a crucial part of any successful business. A key part of brand development comes down to defining what your brand represents. Identifying your target market will help your to define your brand. A brand that is successful creates a unique experience for its customers. The authentic brands know how to communicate with their customers. Redbull use extreme sports to reach their target market. They understand that their customers are young and use a marketing approach that promotes high adrenaline activities which reinforce their tagline *'No Red Bull, no wings'*. They know what language their customers speak. They know what makes their product compelling to the people that experience it. Red Bull's slogan was originally:*'It gives you wings'* until they were hit with a 13 million dollar lawsuit in 2014 as it was proven that the drink actually doesn't give you wings! It was later changed to: *'No Red Bull, no wings'*.

What to Do

Define your brand by defining what your brand stands for and the types of products and services that your customers can expect to receive from your company. Consider how people will think and feel about your business when they have an interaction with your company. Ask yourself what promise you can give over and over to your customers without letting down either them or yourself. Every aspect of your business comes into play here so give great attention to your brand name, quality, pricing, location, people and culture.

Tips and Take Homes

Pick your brand name wisely and design your logo professionally. Your business name and logo will describe your brand better than any words, taglines or testimonial.

Digital Nugget

If your brand is the new kid on the block, market your brand on every platform, blog, and newsfeed you can find. Let people see it continuously. The more they see it the more they will remember it. You will quickly learn what works and what doesn't. Look online for examples of businesses that do branding well and follow their success.

59. PERSONALISE YOUR PRODUCT WITH THE CUSTOMER'S NAME

How it Works

In 2014, having not drank a bottle of coke since 2006, I surrendered to *Coca-Cola's* 'share a coke' campaign in a moment of weakness when I saw my name on a coke bottle in the local super market. It was an instant hypnotic reaction of absolute ownership. They had me. I had to buy it. I felt it was mine. It was calling me and I answered. Coca-Cola customised their product to a personal level and it worked. They gave me emotional possession of something that wasn't even on my shopping list. Years earlier, a similar type of marketing campaign happened when *Barry's Tea* enabled their customers to order custom-made boxes of tea with individual names on them. I had to have a box of *Oisin's Tea*. This is micro marketing on a very intimate level.

What to Do

The first job in treating different customers differently is to acknowledge their individualism. Look at your packaging and timeline for manufacturing of your products. Printing can be done on demand and this can help you create a personalised experience for your client. Examine all points of contact with your customers online and offline. Look for a place where they can be addressed by name. Look at *Starbucks*. They have a simple process of asking each customer their name and writing it on their 'to go' cup. The name is then called out when the order is ready. If you run a restaurant, you have an opportunity to individualise the menu by adding the customer's name. Simply invest in a printer and ask their names on arrival. Print up a templete menu in the moment. If the clients have pre-booked you can have them ready.

Tips and Take Homes

Get good at identifying ways to provide unique greetings. If you don't have a client's name, ask. It's that simple and it's very effective.

Digital Nugget

Collect each individual customer's details where possible. This will allow you to create follow up emails with a personalised message.

60. MAKE A BOLD BRAND PROMISE

How it Works

A brand promise is an attractive promise from you to your customers to do something that ensures that the value that they expect is delivered time after time without fail. It's another reason for them to buy from you. The City Bin Co. brand promise is:

'Job Done! We will do the job right each and every time. You will never have to listen to excuses or sad stories. And should we break our promise then you don't pay.'

A simple message with the reassurance of delivery stating if we mess up, we'll pay up. When you constantly deliver on your brand promise you sow the seeds of a strong philosophy that allows you and your brand to build trust with your customers. They are more than likely to become repeat customers. They are more than likely to tell others about their experience.

What to Do

Craft a brand promise to your customers, which you honestly can stand over. It needs to be strong, clear and simple. Establish a brand promise that your customers will react to and that you can implement and measure. Think about what you are delivering to the customer, how you are going to deliver to the customer and what value you give to the customer. Be bold and keep it unique. It needs to be different from your competitors. If everybody is offering it, it's not a brand promise, it's an added service.

Tips and Take Homes

Don't break your promise. If it breaks for any reason find out why and change it. Go back to the drawing board. Keep your brand promise brief and consistent.

Digital Nugget

Make a banner for your brand promise that can be placed upfront on your landing pages, home page, blogs, email signatures, and social media platforms.

61. POSITION YOUR BRAND WITH EMOTION

How it Works

Positioning your brand can mean many different things to a lot of different people from competitor comparisons to product quality. In my opinion, it's about one thing: Emotion. The emotional connection with your customers will position your brand where you want it to be. Trustworthiness, price, location, words, image and all the other brand facts are simply elements that influence and build the emotional connection.

What to Do

Identify the emotional benefit that your customers receive from using your products. Think about how you want your customers to feel about you every time they think about you. Try to sum up in a phrase what you offer. Think of the famous tagline for L'Oreal that reads, '*Because you're worth it.*' This is an example of a brand positioning by placing value on the emotional coolness that the product portraits. L'Oreal position the brand not just with a tagline, but with a strong emotional undertaking that draws in their clients on the confidence that the brand gives to its users.

Tips and Take Homes

Brand positioning executed with brilliance will allow the uniqueness of your brands to have instant value for clients through instant recognition. Your emotional brand positioning is the small detail that separates you from your competitor. When you see celebrities with household names using your product, speak to them. Look for testimonials that you can use in your promotion.

Digital Nugget

Drive loyalty and build online customer relationships by incorporating elevated echelons of emotional content into your online communications with your customers. Use pictures, text and video.to visually capture the energy of how your customers feel when using your product.

62. GROW YOUR BRAND LIKE A GREAT BIG APPLE TREE

How it Works

I have a great apple tree in my garden. I planted it with my wife when she was expecting our first child and we made sure the soil was right. The environment had to be in the right condition. The timing was important too. My wife's patience, love and care protected the tree by keeping an eye on it daily. Having a nurturing mindset is important when you grow anything. The first year yielded no fruit. The second year we got a handfull. Now, 5 years on, we get between 5 and 10 buckets of the tastiest apples that we give to our neighbours and friends.

What to Do

Think of your business like an apple tree. You mind the tree every day until it can mind itself and, even then, you continue working with it. Growing your brand is no different. You have to give it everything it needs to work and when it is working you repeat the process. The tree my wife and I planted is now big and strong. It keeps giving and giving. We have learned a lot from our first experience and are now ready to plant another. When you grow your brand, you grow it one customer at a time. You give that customer all your attention and look after them. When they are happy with your product then you look after the next customer. Don't attempt to take on too much at the start. Grow one customer at a time. One product at a time and that way it will grow organically like a great big apple tree.

Tips and Take Homes

I tell the apple tree story as it's all about growth. Natural growth. Plan for growth. Keep up with developments in your industry and communicate with your customers. Invest in new technologies and people that will nurture your growth.

Digital Nugget

As you grow offline, stimulate your growth online by increasing your online activities. Create micro sites or landing pages that draw new interest in your next big apple tree!

63. KEEP YOUR BRAND CONSISTENT

How it Works

Keeping your brand consistent is extremely important for your business as it helps establish the image of your company as a tangible brand. It helps bring your brand to the front of your customer's mind through brand recognition. Consistency builds familiarity and helps customers and potential clients remember you. Recognition builds trust, which in turn helps to increase sales. When potential customers feel that they know you, they are more likely to take a chance on your product. Repetition of brand images and messages helps potential customers to get to know your brand.

What to Do

Look at the big brands and study their attention to consistency. Study how they keep the same tone throughout all of their communication. Learn from them. Apply what you learn. Note that it's not just about their logo. Your brand means more than the logo. Think of your style, tone, fonts, voice and the message of your brand. Maintain the consistency of your brand by keeping your logos and company visuals including tone, style and colour consistent with your brand guidelines without exception.

Tips and Take Homes

Brand consistency entails repeating the same communications over and over so they stick in your customer's mind and heart. You won't have to re-create graphics for different social media sites. Keep your graphics up to date on your different social media sites. Keep all your profile pictures, banners, logos and colours on file so you can easily access them when you need them.

Digital Nugget

Place your brand guidelines, official company images, and logos in a downloadable media pack on your website. This enables anybody to have access and download the correct marketing material related to your business. If your brand is misrepresented, you can direct the publisher to the media pack.

64. DISCOVER YOUR BRAND PERSONALITY

How it Works

Is your brand happy, serious, fun and bright or maybe a little conservative? All brands have a personality. Once you discover your brand personality, you can use that information in your marketing efforts. Your communication can be more consistent. Your choices on outlining your brand verbally and visually will be easier to express. Your brand may have many personalities. If you don't define your standout personality you will end up wearing whatever hat suits you on the day. This can confuse customers and be a turnoff for potential buyers.

What to Do?

Develop and use your authentic brand personality to express emotions that enable your clients to link your company to a certain name or feeling. Allow your brand's personality to mirror the personas of your potential customers making it easier for them to relate to your brand. Ask your existing customers how they see you. Simplify the language you use to define your brand personality.

Tips and Take Homes

As with anybody that is true to one's self, allow your brand to sit comfortably in its own skin. Express this through language, tone, feeling and movement of information and channels used.

Digital Nugget

Your online brand personality isn't just the words you use in your social media sites, your website, or the pictures and videos you use on your marketing materials. It's also your customer's emotional reaction to what they experience. The language and tone they use with you on your social media outlets will often be a reflection of the personality gaps between you and the clients.

REV UP YOUR PR ENGINE & BECOME MORE MEDIA SAVVY

The world of PR and media are ever changing with the growth of digital media and real time newsfeeds. You use the media to communicate messages to your audiences. Public relations is often the machine by which you deliver your exciting story. Nowadays, you have more opportunity to manage the movement of information between your business and the public. The purpose of public relations is to educate the public, your customers, non-customers, employees, and all others that may have an interest about certain aspects of your business. This is very different from marketing communication, which amounts to paid advertising. Public relations include undertakings such as anticipating potential viewpoints of the public and addressing any concerns that arise. Successful PR also entails writing professional press releases, managing communication, managing events around product launches and telling the company story to the right audience at the right time. The objective is to bridge the gap between the public view and your company values. You can achieve this by building, and maintaining a relationship with your customers, the media, relevant bloggers, the general public and other influencers.

Before writing and distributing press releases, you have to understand your audience. You have to understand the media. You have to learn how to connect them both. Understand the media machine. Learn how to use it and convert sales with it. Brand awareness starts and ends with increasing sales, in the same way increased revenue hinges on greater brand awareness. Press releases, media and advertising are tools that will drive your story in front of the right eyeballs. Effective PR strategies contain many of the same tricks and tools employed in digital marketing. Think like a journalist. Tell your story often. Don't just be in the audience at networking events. It's better to be a professional speaker telling your story to the audience. When using suitable media to tell your story and to send messages to your audience, don't just think digital and print; think television, radio and outdoor media for the wider audience. Think about going door-to-door and street-by-street for the local audience.

Using media and public relations is an invaluable way to build brand awareness and gain new clients. Spend time and energy designing and planning a strategy to get your business known. Put your brand in front of as many people as possible. Rev up your own PR engine and work the media machine regularly.

65. WRITE A PROFESSIONAL PRESS RELEASE

How it Works

A press release is the tool used to get your story into the different media channels, be it the pages of the newspaper, a daytime chat show on TV or an online platform. You can use this format to announce just about anything from the launch of a business, a new product, to an award won or a new partnership. A press release is a golden ticket to an attentive audience; but it is only gold if you send the right message to the right people at the right time. The newsrooms of every media company get numerous press releases every day from thousands of people telling their unique tear-jerking story, companies launching innovating products and organisations looking for funding. All are in competition hoping that their press release will be picked up and circulated to the masses. You are competing for space with your competitors, non-competitors and identities that have the financial power to buy the space. Excellent content and narrative stands out and will interest both the target audience and the media outlets best-equipped to reach them.

What to Do

Be clear and consistent when telling your story and delivering your message. Stick to the facts. If it's not relevant it shouldn't be in there. Be clear with your words on your press release. Be creative with the packaging of it. Don't just stick it in a white envelope and post it. Do something that stands out. Get their attention before they even open it. Before launching my first book *The Binman's Guide to Selling*, I delivered advanced readers copies of the books to selected journalists and media outlets in a pizza box style packaging. When the box was opened the book was sitting on red shredded paper with the press release & cover letter bookmarking the content page. Local, national and global media outlets picked up on the press release and the story. The press release was distinctive. I made sure that it would stand out from all the other press releases sitting on the desks of media researchers. It communicated the story behind the product and did not just focus on the product. The headline said exactly what was on the tin.

Have a clear title with a hook that catches attention. Put all your important information on the top of the first few paragraphs. The media outlet may not be in a position to print it all. They will generally chop from the bottom up if they go to make it shorter. I suggest writing 200 to 300 words in the body.

Make sure you say everything that you need to say in the body of text. Studying Public Relations at The Irish Academy of PR taught me to ensure I always had the *who, where, what, when, why* and *how* of the story. Don't get flowery with fancy words. Keep it simple and to the facts. Include a relevant quote to back up your information. After the text of the main body write ENDS. This tells the editors to only publish what's above ENDS. Under this you have what is called a *boilerplate*. This is where you can give a bit of background information and your contact details.

Here are two examples press releases. The first is for the local launch of my first book *'The Binman's Guide to Selling'*.

PRESS RELEASE
For immediate use

Talking Rubbish?

Bin man turns life lessons into winning sales techniques with the launch of an internationally praised business book.

23 May 2013: *A former bin man has today launched his first book detailing 100 winning sales techniques, which have seen the company he works for experience 18% sales growth year-on-year.*

Oisín Browne, author of The Binman's Guide to Selling, started out as a second helper on The City Bin Co.'s early morning bin collection route in Galway back in 1998. Rising up through the ranks over the past 15 years, he has seen the company grow from a handful of employees with one truck, two customers and four bins in Galway, to over 100 staff in Ireland and ambitious plans for Europe.

Now a shareholder in the company who works in the sales and marketing team, Browne's book charts the lessons learned over the years in bite-sized tips to help guide the budding entrepreneur or salesman, or anyone seeking inspiration to get into a winning mindset.

Speaking at the launch, Browne said: "Working on the truck was akin to the classroom. Starting at any time between 3am and 6am in the morning and working in all conditions, I learned the importance of time management and teamwork. I was exercising every day and keeping myself fit without even knowing it. Eight hours a day running after a big truck and picking up rubbish tends to do that."

Browne added: "The book contains something for everyone – from students, to business and sales management teams, to the curious person studying at The University of Life."

An accessible and informative read, The Binman's Guide to Selling's key chapters include 'Don't Drop Your Trousers!'; 'The Secret Language of Selling'; and 'Break The Year Down To The Day.' Littered with colourful, real-life anecdotes and accompanying tips, the book also contains interviews with top-selling teams, business owners and consultants, including Fyffes, Maxol and RTÉ Radio.

Launching the book, entrepreneur and former Dragon's Den panelist, Seán Gallagher said: 'The Binman's Guide to Selling is more than just an account of how to succeed in business. Where many business motivation books merely recycle old formulae, Browne, though a series of evidence-based pointers effortlessly dispels myths and steers readers on a direct course to personal success. This is a business guide, lifestyle tool and humorous read all in one."

The Binman's Guide to Selling is available on Amazon.com
Visit **www.binmansguide.com**

****

ENDS

Notes to Editors

For more information on the book or to arrange an interview
with author of *The Binman's Guide to Selling,* Oisín Browne, please
contact: **info@binmansguide.com** or phone **1800-CITYBIN**
The second Press Release is announcing averda's acquisition of a majority
stake in leading South African waste management group, Wasteman
Holdings (Pty) Ltd.

PRESS RELEASE
For immediate use

**Averda Enters South African Waste Management Market
Majority Stake Acquisition of Wasteman Holdings Announced Today**

April 2015: Averda, the largest provider of integrated waste management solutions across the emerging world, has announced today its acquisition of a majority stake in leading South African waste management group, Wasteman Holdings (Pty) Ltd. averda will take a majority share in Wasteman, expanding averda's footprint in Africa alongside its other international operations and providing a solid platform for further growth in the continent.

Wasteman is one of the largest waste management companies in South Africa and has operated for 35 years providing fully integrated solutions to leading industry sectors on a national basis. The investment brings significant advantages to both businesses with the opportunity to leverage various initiatives and experiences around city cleaning, waste disposal and recycling as well as the development around new and innovative waste management programmes.

The Chairman of averda, Maysarah Sukkar, commented: "In line with our global growth ambitions, the acquisition of Wasteman significantly enhances averda's position in Africa to provide specialised solutions for waste management. We are excited about the opportunity ahead and look forward to bringing our vast international experience from city cleaning to waste recovery and disposal to Wasteman's operations."

Jan Labuschagne, CEO of Wasteman Holdings (Pty) Ltd remarked: "Wasteman group will reap immense benefit from the entry of averda into the South African market. In addition to the injection of foreign direct investment, averda will contribute a wealth of waste industry expertise and technology. We look forward to partnering with our new majority shareholder along a path of accelerated growth."

****

ENDS
Notes to Editors

About averda: *averda International is the largest environmental solutions provider in the MENA region, specializing in integrated resources management. averda is at the forefront of innovation in the regional market, providing sustainable solutions and more than 35 years of experience in the effective management of waste for both private and public sector clients across pedestrian, residential, commercial and industrial areas. averda's extensive portfolio of services ranges from street cleaning through to waste collection, treatment, disposal and recycling. The company's capabilities also include the development of solutions for water, wastewater and solid waste of public, residential, commercial, and industrial sectors, all within a sustainable framework that respects the natural environment. averda also designs and implements full-scale solutions to recover valuable and recyclable resources like paper, metals, and water. Serving in excess of 9 million people every day, averda operates in full compliance with international standards for quality control throughout Lebanon, Saudi Arabia, the United Arab Emirates, Oman, Qatar, the Republic of Ireland, Morocco, Angola, Jordan and Gabon.*

Contact

CONTACT
Philippa Charlton
800 averda
www.averda.com

****

Both press releases were published in local, national and international media outlets online and offline.

Tips and Take Homes

Have a local focus headline that communicates your main point. Say it in one line. Be sure to include a professional photograph. Put your contact details at the end. Let the editor know you have a press release/photo attached and be sure to invite them and their photographer to the event product launch. Invite them to meet you for an exclusive one on one interview. Call the person to let them know you are sending them a press release. Follow up by contacting them a few days later. Ask them if they can use it.

If they say they can't, ask them if they can share their thoughts on the piece. This allows you to build a profile of the content type that they use for future press releases. It helps you to build relationships. Follow the editors and media outlets on Twitter, Facebook and LinkedIn. Communicate with them on these social channels. This is a great way to build rapport and for them to learn a little more about who you are and what you do.

Digital Nugget

Use video links on your press releases that will allow the reader to click through to supporting information and sources. Include links to websites, photos, articles that are applicable to your story. Double-check that all relevant files are attached to your email before sending and that spelling and grammar are correct.

66. THINK LIKE A PROFESSIONAL JOURNALIST

How it Works

A great marketing mindset predates expert marketing. Journalists have long embraced the skills later applied by marketers and advertisers to create engaging and beneficial content. They instinctively go out and look for the story. They research their story and they write great content. They know their reader's demographic and narrate the message for their audience. A great reporter can instinctively place himself or herself into the reader's shoes in the same way that a great marketer needs to learn to be in the potential client's shoes. Whether you're part of a multinational company or a sole trader, content marketing requires a creative person who knows how to collect information, do product history analysis, build relationships with customers, and carry out fact-finding missions. You must learn where to get first, second and third hand consumer feedback. Once all this information is collected, the magic is in putting it all together to create something special. You are aiming to create amazing content that will hook the audience in a way that brings them back for more.

What to Do

Hire a journalist as part of your marketing, PR and social media team. If that is not possible, you need to get out from the office and look for the story. You are not just looking for a story that will be pleasing to your social media audience, local media or your logo-loving ego. You need to provide valued material that will be seen as a benefit to your industry, other industries, online sites, and even your competitors! Start by going to your local newspaper and offer to write a topic focus column, which will be of value to you, the newspaper and the reader. Also, start a blog. This can be separate to your business blog. It can be on a topic that allows you to be or become an expert in a certain field. For example, if you sell baby products, write a mother and baby advice column. If you are an accountant you could write tips for good home bookkeeping and money management. If you sell farming equipment, write for the farming supplements about best farming practices and product reviews. Offer to contribute to newspapers, blogs, local newsletters or thought leadership whitepapers.

Contact businesses that have strong reputable blogs and strong social media platforms. Invite them to interview you about your story for their blog. They are also looking for content! Look to guest blog on blogs that are established and influential. Decide how often you wish to create content. Create a content calendar to help you plan each story idea. Writing is a skill that takes time, from idea generation, looking for the story, to writing, drafting, editing, publishing and sharing the story. The key objective is that you are speaking to your target market about subjects that interest and help them. This may not be your product; however, maybe it is linked indirectly to what you sell. In doing so, you are establishing a network. You are writing regularly. When you are writing you need to research. If you are researching you are learning. You are networking a particular community through your online presence so that when they have a need for your services you will be on their radar. The door will be opened. The familiarity of your name will be warm and the sale will come naturally.

Tips and Take Homes

Place all that is appealing to your past, present and future customers, at the centre of your marketing efforts when writing content. The best way to do this is with the mindset of a great journalist. Make your content as valuable as possible. Show that you value the person reading it: your existing clients and potential customers.

Digital Nugget

Content marketing is more than just keywords and links. It's about increasing awareness of your business and brand. If you focus on quality and relevant content, ultimately you will draw interest and loyalty from your audiences and build a valuable online community whom you can call on to share your content.

67. ADD SALES CHARM TO YOUR ADVERTS

How it Works

When you place an advert in the local newspaper or the national broadsheets, you may have romantic notions about potential clients going online and ordering your products right away. The phone will be hopping mad and your products will be growing legs and running out the door as you sleep. It doesn't happen that easy! However, there are many simple techniques that can be applied to your advert so that the reader knows you are there. You have to add sales charm to your creative process. Yes, you want a sale! You want to be seen. You want to create brand awareness. You want the advert to ultimately lead to more sales. If you are a baker you are not only competing with every other baker who has an advert in the newspaper. You are competing with every other business that has an advert for the x amount of money in the readers' pockets, which may be zero as they may have already spent their last few cents on the paper that they are reading and the coffee they are drinking. Or it may be that they have money but the business with the catchy advert on the radio caught their attention at the right time. The best way to get a result with newspaper readers is to be in the paper in the first place. **If you are not in, you can't win**. Don't just plan your advert to be published once. A once-off advert will not work. You want the reader who is your potential client to see your advert every time they open the newspaper because you stand out from the noise and you catch their attention by being cleverly different.

What to Do

Work within your budget. Twelve business card size adverts once a month can be more valuable than one or two full-page adverts printed each year. Numerous small adverts generate as much great sales as big adverts. Why? It's not about size. It's about the consistency and placement of your message. It is the ability to connect with the reader. It can take up to a dozen times for a reader to visually connect and recognise your advert. Make sure your advert reflects your business, brand and unique offering using a simple one-line message. Lay out your advert so that its appearance gives the same look or feeling each time it is published. Design a distinctive logo to use in every print advert that is unique to you. Look at the colour and tone of the newspaper you are using. If all other adverts are in colour, design your advert in black and white or visa-versa. Use a unique phone number and email on all adverts.

This allows you to track the conversion rate of your advert campaign, make changes as you go and negotiate your long-term prices with the paper.

Tips and Take Homes

Look at having your adverts connected to local events, national holidays, and the weather. The City Bin Co. would always put their advert for skips in print if the weather man had predicted a sunny week ahead and if it was cloudy or raining there would have a different offering. Dictate the advert location within the paper. Think about your advert positioning in the newspaper. If you see a match between you and a certain section such as sports, current affairs, business or entertainment, ask for your advert to be placed in that section. Request that your advert to be placed on the same page in every publication. This creates familiarity with the reader, as you will own that space in every issue and over time the reader will know where to find you. If you are very adventurous ask for your advert to be printed upside down. This will allow you to stand out!

Digital Nugget

Share your adverts that appear in traditional media outlets on your blogs. Write about the process of taking out an advert and why you choose a certain message.

68. CHAMPION A CHARITY

How it Works

To champion a charity is to help people on all sorts of levels. The way businesses and charities work together has changed and developed the social responsibility field in such a way that the emphasis is on more than money and donations. The fundamental aim is to find a charity that can benefit from your skills, products, and people. Your brand can get value by helping and being associated with their name. Such a partnership helps to market your brand and build awareness of the organisation. It is a great way to develop an influential network and help with a good cause in the process. People like to affiliate themselves with companies that support causes and charities in a positive meaningful manner. It is a credible way to connect with your own customers and potential clients. It's great to give. It's good to be seen to be giving and it's fantastic for the recipient who receives the support.

What to Do

Locate a charity that fits well with your business. Look at its goals. Look at their support systems. If you don't already champion a charity start by issuing a press release to all charities in your area stating that you are looking for a charity to work with for one year. You will get significant of interest. Go and meet with the different charities. What can you offer them? What can they offer you? Pick one charity and run with them for one year. Collectively decide on a mutual goal for that year. Design a partnership plan. Document every success, event and learning from the partnership with blogs, photos, videos and press releases. Charities, like businesses, are interested in building awareness and any marketing of events, associated blogs or press releases that highlight the partnership will be welcomed. Include your charitable participation in all marketing materials such as newsletters, brochures, signs, displays, advertisements, and commercials. Make sure to ask your charity to do the same for your business. Ask the charity to acknowledge your support in their promotional activities on their website, blog and marketing material.

You could also change the charity after one or two years. This makes everything fresh and new. Learning from year one will benefit your activity and partnership in year two and so forth. Also, it gives new marketing opportunities to both parties.

Do something different. In 2015 The City Bin Co. created an innovative project called *Giving Day* or *BinPact* as it's known internally. Using a digital social-sharing platform called *in/PACT* the company shared its social responsibility with the all employees. Every Sunday an email is sent out to all employees giving them the opportunity to donate a certain amount of money on the company's behalf to their charity of choice. In the few months since its introduction, The City Bin Co.'s employees had pledged over $6,000 to 32 deserving charities. The charities themselves have embraced this initiative, and recognise that this is a powerful tool in their fundraising activity. One aspect that is particularly important is the ability to share the activity on social platforms, which the charities can then repost or retweet, broadening the reach and engaging many more people. Mike Carty, of Blood Bike West, one of the charities that recieves contributions from the employees send an email to The City Bin Co. after the first month to say: *'Many thanks to yourself and all the staff in The City Bin Co. for your donations to Blood Bike West over the last month. Your donations covered half the fuel bill for our bikes last month. This helps us keep our bikes on the road saving lives and money for our cash strapped Hospitals.'* It impacts employees directly and shows employees that what they're doing goes beyond the money. It makes a difference directly in their lives and in the issues they care about. Every company should have a weekly Giving Day! How can you create your company *Giving Day*?

Tips and Take Homes

You can give special discounts to your clients who are connected with your chosen charity or give a token percentage of each transaction to the charity. See where you can be of real value and support by bringing your business knowledge, networking contacts, people resources, assets, skills and unique corporate understandings to the core of the charity. Niamh Bray of The City Bin Co. has sat on the Board of Directors of *Hand in Hand* children cancer charity for 6 years. We branded the side of our trucks with the charities logos and placed their brand on our letterheads. This all helped in bringing awareness to our clients about the charity.

Digital Nugget

Develop an online counter or register that shows the work done and contributions made to the charity. This keeps the connection transparent and creates a real time account of events for people to follow.

69. REDESIGN YOUR BUSINESS CARD

How it Works

A well-designed and good quality business card will make you and your business look professional. Though it is a modest instrument in marketing your business, it can be the starting point for some of your most successful sales outcomes. A business card is a marketing tool that represents your first point of contact. It tells people you want to do business and how you can be of service. How can it stand out from the thousands of business cards out there? An amazing business card needs to be designed to attract and draw new customers to your product. If you are not giving everybody you meet your business card, you are not selling. If it is not getting you business, it is not working. Most business cards end up in the bin. This does not mean that they do not have a purpose; it is a sign that they have served their purpose and have been used or that they weren't a great business card to grab anybody's attention. The age of business cards is changing as the digital age is shaping how we give and receive our little pocket billboard that says who we are, what we do and how to contact us. The purpose of a business card is not just to make you more contactable. Let's face it; the person you give it to already has your details. They more than likely got it all before you met since you are connected with them on your professional networking site. I'm sure they would have already checked you out! The value is in the giving of a small token of appreciation. The offering is a chance to wow the person on the receiving end of your well designed and eye catching business cards. It's another interaction for anybody in your company looking to do business with a potential client. Every point of contact reinforces the familiarity of the brand, the service, the personal assertiveness and commitment of those who are exchanging details. It is a chance to build rapport.

In 2013, I attended the European Business Awards function at the British Embassy in Dublin. I was receiving the certificate for the National Champion in Customer Service for The City Bin Co. It was a great night for networking as the room was full of representatives who had entered the competition. The nominees came from all corners of Ireland. They were the best of the best in business. They were networking and making introductions. Business cards were changing hands. I always have my business cards with me; however, on this particular evening I had left them back at the office. Not one to be left out, I decided to give the people a bookmarker instead.

I had bookmarkers printed up for my first book *The Binman's Guide to Selling* as promotional gifts. There were no details on it other than the website for the book. It became a great conversation starter throughout the night. So successful was it that I went to the local printer the next day and asked them to put my traditional-looking business card and the bookmarker together. To this day, I use it. It acts as a great icebreaker. The trick is to be different. Create something that will be consistent with your brand yet stand out from the crowd.

What to Do

Start by laying out all the business cards you have that belong to others on a table. Place your card along side them. Make a note of all their similarities from their size, to the quality, the content, colour, cut and images. Now redesign your card to be everything that the others are not. Redesign your business card to be a calling card and a conversation starter. Think about placing a picture or image underneath the text or on the back of the card that will stimulate emotions and get people talking about it. Be different with the shape. Could it be the shape of your logo or your product? Could your card have a secondary use such as a bookmarker? Change the size. Don't settle for the standard size. Cards that fold in half or tri-fold can be like mini-brochures and hold a little more information such as discounts, customer testimonials and product reviews. The cost of business cards is very competitive within the printing industry nowadays. It is a great idea to redesign and update the company business cards once a year.

Tips and Take Homes

Always double-check the copy on the proof before going to print. There is nothing more embarrassing then giving a potential client your card with a typo. Yes, it would be different but not in the way you want.

Digital Nugget

Create a virtual follow up version of your business card that can be emailed out to all people that give you their business cards to acknowledge your interaction with them. Insert your business card into your email signature.

70. LAUNCH IT LIKE NASA

How it Works

When I launched my first book in May 2013, I didn't stop launching it. I first launched it at Charlie Byrne's bookstore in the west of Ireland. Then I launched it in the east, the south and the north of Ireland. I launched it online. I launched it in business groups up and down the country. I have launched it in businesses. I launched it in the newspapers and on the radio. I launched it in other languages. When I launch this, my second book, I will re-launch the first book alongside it.

When you launch something frequently, you become an expert at event and product launching. You write press release after press release and learn to create a buzz about you, your business, your brand and your products. It becomes the norm. There are so many opportunities to plug business elements yet each affords you scope to be unique whether it's launching a business venture at the outset, introducing new products and staff, to relaunches and anniversaries. When you build awareness through product launch repetition, you learn what works, where to expand and what to drop. Launching anything in business means putting a public focus on that particular subject and getting people excited about it. You may have done it when your business first opened. Have you done it since? What would happen if you did it on a frequently? You would become an expert at launching your products.

What to Do

Make an events calendar around your business and products. Plan a launch for a specific line of products. Invite your customers. Invite well-known local people. Organise some finger food and light refreshments. I believe every business can do this no matter what the product. Issue a press release the week before to all your existing customers, local media and online bloggers. Hire a photographer so that you have photos to accompany the before and after press release to the media. These photos can also be used as content for your online platforms. Invite a local musician to play bit of music. Invite the local mayor to say a few words. Make it a big deal. Launch it like NASA every time.

Tips and Take Homes

Launches work when you have the preparation hours clocked up and everything double-checked. Create a launch checklist that you can apply to any launch within your business. Build your customer database. These are the guys who will keep coming back and supporting you. Give bonuses, discounts and samples on the night. Have a raffle and great giveaway. Tell the story of why you are in business and why you sell what you sell. This is what connects you to the people that show up at your launches. Keep the launches to a minimum size. It's better to have a small room with 20 people in it then a big room with the same 20 people making the room look empty.

Digital Nugget

Live stream the launch so that people who cannot come to the event can attend from afar! Make such to share a short sharable story at your launch that will appeal to the people you are watching the live stream. Place the camera in a good location that will catch the atmosphere of the launch. When they are watching it on their laptop you want they to feel like they are part of it. Do this by acknowledging them. Once you have the recording you can upload a video trailer of the event and post an audio sound bite of the launch to your social media pages.

71. SIGN UP FOR A PROFESSIONAL GRAMMAR COURSE

How it Works

You cannot talk to everybody all the time, so how you communicate is crucial in conveying the most professional and personable impression you can. Missing words, spelling errors, poor punctuation and meandering sentences are all too common in business today. If you don't practice good grammar, you won't have it. It may or may not be evident but spelling and grammar are of the greatest importance when it comes to marketing. No one is perfect and I certainly hold my hand up as guilty of typos, missing words, repeated words and other errors. That's why I completed a grammar course and can communicate the benefits.

As a marketer, you will be writing more press releases, content for blogs and proposals for projects than you can imagine. Without an editor on hand to correct every little grammatical error, you will need to brush up on your own professional grammar skills. With the over-use of abbreviated text and auto-spelling, the standards can drop if a watchful and knowledgeable eye isn't cast over outbound material. Bad grammar, or misunderstood writing, can be reason enough for your material not to get published or your projects not to get the thumbs up. Simple misunderstandings due to poor grammar can be costly to put right both in lost opportunities, money and staff time.

What to Do

Learn the mechanics of sentence structure. Study punctuation. Relearn nouns and pronouns, adjectives and verbs. Become familiar with the nitty-gritty participles, gerunds, prepositions and conjunctions. Yes, you can say you already know these and I don't doubt it but laziness and everyday distractions can result in disaster. See your practice as fine-tuning. Learn to evaluate your sentences. Is there a better way to say it? Is there a word that needs to be deleted or added? In short, can you express yourself accurately, concisely and imaginatively? The more you attempt this, the better you will get. Practice makes perfect.

Tips and Take Homes

Always have a colleague read over your press releases, reports and any other content. By the time you've completed your writing task, you may not be able to see your own mistakes. You are not asking for a rewrite, just a quick human spellcheck. Again, the more you do this the less you will need to do it. Missing words and other blunders may not be apparent to your eyes; but a fresh pair of eyes can find them and point them out to you.

Digital Nugget

Sign up for an online course on grammar for business, there are numerous resources available. Document your learning experience on a blog post. There is no shame in sharpening your skills. This way, you can encourage others to do the same and raise the standards of marketing one marketer at a time!

72. START PROFESSIONAL SPEAKING

How it Works

Storytelling is a big part of marketing and selling. Tap into the art of professional speaking to build confidence in storytelling and in presenting your product and brand. Reach out to all business groups, large corporate, communities, universities and interest groups. Ask to speak at their events. Tell your story. Don't advertise or blindly promote a product.

Don't sell; tell. Tell people why you are in business. Tell them techniques you have learned on your marketing journey that may work for them. Tell them your failures. Tell them your successes. Share the knowledge. Engage with them. If you connect with them they will look to learn more about you and what you do.

You can network in a room full of prospects and get one or two contacts or you can be the focus of that room and get everybody's attention. In May 2013, I joined the Professional Speaking Association. I have never looked back. I quickly learned if I am going to put myself in front of an audience, I needed to learn the art of professional speaking. I learned how to engage, how to craft a story and how to deliver a talk. Professional speaking is the ultimate networking tool that will spread your brand story far and wide.

What to Do

Spend time to plan and design your talk. Have a specialised subject matter that tells your story yet gives your audience something to take away and apply to their own situation. This could be social media, online sales or the five big things you learned from your small failures in business. To find this message look for the common thread. People generally remember one message from talks they attend. More is remembered if the talk is enthusiastically delivered. Give your talk a catchy title. I have three different talks that I present. Each talk has a single message. My first talk is titled: **The Binman's Guide to Selling**. The message is '*Sales: If you don't ask you don't get.*' My 2nd talk is titled **From The Bin Truck to the Boardroom.** The message is '*Get motivated to move up*' and my third talk is **Beyond Visualization** and the message is '*Turning visions into actions.*'

Before going out and telling your story, practice in front of a selected audience. Ask for their feedback. Chop and change your talk until you are happy and until you see that it works and gets a positive reaction.

Tips and Take Homes

Start with a story that immediately captures the attendee's attention. Learn to deliver with or without slides. Keep your talk to an agreed time. Leave your contact details for follow up calls and ask everybody for details by sending around a sign-in sheet. Connect with the people by having interactive parts of your talk, for example, do a show of hands or a quick round the room two-line introduction.

Digital Nugget

Record all your talks so you can use them online as an example of your expertise in your field. Ask all attendees for a testimonial that you can place on your webpage.

73. WELCOME CUSTOMERS TO THE CLUB!

How it Works

The transaction can often be the last point of contact for most businesses and customers. Business people cannot afford to sit back and hope for the best when it comes to repeat business. You cannot predict if a client will return. You can say good-bye when a customer leaves or you can be proactive in turning that good bye into a buy-in from your customer.

What to Do

Create a community of diehard fans. Create a customer relationship building process where your customers can feel part of a welcoming community. Don't just take their hard-earned cash and let them walk out the door. Create online training programs that teach the client how to get the best from the product. Start an online forum where you and the users can meet each other. They can communicate in real time about successes and problems that they have with your product. Create a league table for the best users of your product that encourages all users to be in the top 10. Give the users a cool club or community name. Let it be a place where they can get limited edition products, discounts and brand memorabilia.

Tips and Take Homes

When people sign up for a club, the expectation is that they will receive something or be invited somewhere. Opening a door to an empty room is not inviting. Make things flow, so there is something tangible for your customers to receive on top of a 'thank you' for the money. Consider organising events, promotions and monthly online meetings and forums for your customers to be a part of. Think about parties or get togethers where you focus is on their interests.

Digital Nugget

Create an automated online portal that invites the client to sign up and become part of the community where they get rewards for using your product. When a new guest visits the Hilton Hotel for the first time they automatically get a welcome email that states '*Welcome to the Club*'. Through the 'Hilton HHonors' club they can earn points for free stays and other small perks such as free breakfast and room upgrades. The customer is not just a guest; they are part of the Hilton family!

74. TELL YOUR STORY, TELL IT AGAIN, AND HAMMER IT HOME

How it Works

When Pat Divilly of Pat Divilly Fitness tells the story of how he started his business on a beach, he never goes off script. He tells the same story over and over again. Pat knows that his rags to riches story connects with every single human being that has a dream. He brings people on a journey that repeatedly drives home the message; if Pat can do it anybody can do it. He makes you want to be part of his success and his drive to reach for the stars. More importantly, Pat wants to help you reach your goals as part of the unwritten contract that you help him reach his goals. His story is short and simple. He turns *can't* into *can*.

In May 2012 after leaving the restaurant where he was working, Pat started 'Pat Divilly Fitness.' Broke and depressed, he remembers promising himself that he was going to turn things around. He door-dropped 5000 flyers advertising a boot camp on Silverstrand beach in the West of Ireland. Pat has never looked back. He commits every waking minute to growing his business. That's Pat's story. Short, sweet and simple. He tells it every chance he gets. Since then, there has been a studio launch, two bestselling books, a DVD, work with national TV and radio; he has worked with Facebook HQ, and won multiple awards.

What to Do

Firstly, define your story. Think about the real reason behind why you are doing what you do. Keep it short and to the point. Look for the emotional connection that your potential client will connect with. Write it down and tell it to everybody. Pat Divilly made a personal goal to deliver his story in over 100 seminars around the country in 2014 so he could connect and share his story. This is networking and word-of-mouth marketing at its best. Don't tell a different story every time you communicate. Tell your story and stick to it. Tell it with plenty of passion and energy.

Tips and Take Homes

The more you tell your story, the more you will perfect it; so keep telling it. By repeating it over and over you gain more confidence in your delivery and attract new audiences.

Tell it once. Tell it twice and hammer it home again and again. Get other people to tell it for you.

Digital Nugget

Publish your story on your website, on your blog, on your social media sites. Tell your story on other people's blogs. Do this by commenting on their stories and their blogs that interest you and are related to your product or industry in some way. When you introduce yourself, follow your introduction with your brief story. Get out to networking groups, community groups and business groups and tell your story.

75. TV, RADIO, OUTDOOR AND PRINT

How it Works

TV did not kill the radio star, rather it enhanced it! It is another way into the home of the potential client with a direct call to action. If you have the budget there is nothing like TV, radio and outdoor adverts to bring you visibility, credibility and profitability.

Before The City Bin Co.'s first television advert in 2012, one of our strongest objections from potential customers was *'I won't give you a go because I've never heard of you.'* As soon as the advert aired, this doubt vanished and was replaced by an instant sense of trust and familiarity. There was a new belief that said if you were on TV you must be ok. The radio ads and outdoor billboards have the same effect.

What to Do

Although TV, radio, outdoor and print are very different mediums, any creative process needs attention to detail in the preparation and planning stage. If you do not have the expertise, employ the best creative team. Look for people within your industry, outside your industry and from the academic sphere to give your idea generation a wide-angle view.. They have a huge reach so your message has to be catchy, simple and very clear. Tap into the emotional charge of your potential clients when designing your creative message.

Prolong your campaign by starting with only billboards for 2 weeks. Then, roll out the radio adverts for 2 weeks. After that, introduce the TV advert for 2 weeks. This way, you can measure the impact of each call to action as they go live on the different mediums. On week 6, if your budget allows, push all 3 mediums together for a period to maximise impact and drive your message home. You can run print adverts throughout the whole campaign to support each medium.

As with many marketing tools there can be a cost. These mediums come with a big price tag and are not for every business. It you are going to use them you need to understand the monetary effect this will have on the financial part of your marketing. If is beyond your budget it is good to learn and know the workings of such platforms. It can help you understand your competitors spending if they are using them.

Tips and Take Homes

When creating the typical 30-second advert for TV and radio, do something different. Create a 20 second segment with a 10 second tail end. This way you can ask for the first part to go out at the start of the commercial break and the tail end with the reminder message to go out 2 or 3 adverts later.

Digital Nugget

Make a fly-on-the wall video clip about the making of your TV advert. Interview the actors and director. Film the billboards being put up and taken down. Create a visual for the radio advert. These little video clips will create content that will give you the opportunity to stretch out your campaign online by sharing on your social media platforms. Document and share your whole experience of generating the ideas and the successes of your campaign once it's over. This brings your brand into the thought leadership space of the business world where others can learn from you.

76. GO DOOR TO DOOR

How it Works

One of the best ways to get into every potential customer's home is to go door to door. You can deliver a personalised and geographically focused message. You can do it in the form of a leaflet drop, and, even better if time is on your side, a personal visit. The great thing about marketing your product door to door is that it can cost you as little or as much as you want. Your leaflets can be anything from a personal hand written note to a glossy booklet. By getting face-to-face and one to one with the client, you can collect information speedily and make decisions on the spot. Back in college I spent my summer days and evenings in my final year selling poetry door-to-door. I always started by selecting an area and then, a day or two before calling, I would deliver a short handwritten note with an introduction, what I was doing and why I was doing it. The note said the following:

"My name is Oisin. I am a local student putting myself through college. To do this I create and sell poems. Here is my webpage and contact number. Contact me before the end of this month for a special discount!'

Two days later I would follow up with a door-to-door call. The result was amazing. I sold over 5000 poems in 3 months and earned enough money to pay my rent for an entire year.

What to Do

Select a different target area for each week. This way you can also measure success in each area. This helps in redesigning your message where it has the least traction and gives you a good idea for successful retargeting.

Have your message tailored to the area and a call to action with an end date. For example

"Dublin, Sign up before the end of this July and save 20 percent! Or 'Hi my name is John, I live locally here in Marino and I clean chimneys. Book your chimney to be cleaned before this Friday andbe in with a chance to win a 40kg bag of smokeless coal!"

Once your message has been delivered follow up with a door-to-door call within two days. Introduce yourself and the company you represent by saying:

"Good evening Sir, I am John from 'The Every Home Needs One Company'. I am following up on the note I delivered to you a few days ago. Have you a minute?"

If it's not a good time or the potential customer is not interested, thank them for their time and move on to the next number on the list. Write the response of each potential client down. This enables you to build up a picture of what works and doesn't work in your campaign.

Tips and Take Homes

If you are calling to the homes of other people, dress well and be presentable. Always smile and if you only remember one thing from this book (And I do hope you remember so much more!) let it be the following: **Respect their response**. It's a good idea to have an identification card with your name, photo, logo and contact details.

Digital Nugget

Feature the offers that you are delivering on your website. Enable potential clients to book online. Mention your web address on all leaflets and promotional material. This empowers your potential customer to do the work and to investigate a little more into your background and that of your company.

77. RUN COOL COMPETITIONS

How it Works

Competitions are a great way to engage with customers in a fun manner. Everybody loves to be a winner. The City Bin Co. had a colouring competition a few years ago included in the Christmas newsletter. The prize was a trip to Lapland to visit Santa Claus. There was a great response with thousands of entries received. We have had creative photography competitions on our social media platforms inviting participants to creatively place bins in unusual places and yes, photograph manipulation tools were allowed! The prize was a year's free waste collection. The result of the competition produced great content with the companys' iconic red bins being placed in famous paintings and in well-known locations. One of my preferred photographs was a bin winning a race with Usain Bolt coming second!

What to Do

It needs to be fun. It's not just for the people taking part. It's also for the people observing the results. Let it be as simple as possible. Say what it is. Say whom it is for and say what the prize is. Always have a closing date to create a sense of urgency. Use your product as prizes and if this is not possible, ask your customers about their interests and hobbies. This allows you to gauge what would be a suitable prize that will attract people to enter your competitions. If your competition is a success, repeat it annually. Keep it cool!

Tips and Take Homes

Promote the competition by sending out a newsletter to your email database with a hook in the subject line that will grab their attention.

Digital Nugget

Document photographs and videos of the participants and overall winners on all your social media channels. For example, if you run an art competition, don't just share the contributions of the winners, share all the works of art! You could even invite your followers on social media to pick the winner!

78. GET INTO GUERRILLA MARKETING

How it Works

Guerrilla Marketing focuses on low-cost or no-cost unconventional marketing that generates high brand awareness. Jay Conrad Levinson created the term in his 1984 book *Guerrilla Advertising*. It demands a lot of creativity, energy and time. What you will not need is a big budget. If you are spending big bucks, it is not guerrilla marketing. Think surprise, innovation, creative graffiti, sticker bombing, flash mobs, and unexpected circumstances. Imagine a wheelie bin placed on a busy street and every time a person goes to throw some trash into it a person jumps up with a bunch of flowers.

What to Do

Create a buzz. Your goal is to create something that's extraordinary enough to hook people's attention. You don't want them just to remember it, you want them to talk about it and share the experience. You need to put yourself in experimental mode. Be clear on your overall message and connection with your brand. Make a genuine list of where you want the fruits of your efforts to be seen. Is it a 'have to be there to see it' in the moment thing? Is it traditional media or social media outlets that you would use and benefit from? Where will you get maximum exposure with your guerrilla-marketing ideas? And will it have the right audience? Be visible to the right people.

Tips and Take Homes

Document everything you do on video. The footage can be edited down and made into cool content for your social media platforms. Ask local and national media to be a part of your plan in telling the story from the start.

Digital Nugget

Grow your plan by posting, sharing and blogging before, during and after the campaign kicks off on all your social media channels. Post in 'real time' as events are happening and not a week later when the boat has sailed.

79. DIG DEEP INTO THE DATA

How it Works

In this fast paced age where *Amazon* knows what books you might like to read, *Netflix* recommends movies you'd like to watch, and social media platforms suggest friends you might know, you need to become customer centric. You need to understand these customers from an up close viewpoint without invading their personal space. Your developed products need to land in the viewpoint of your customer because there is an above average fit and not because you put it out there and were hoping for the best. The more detail you have about your target market, the more direct your marketing efforts. Look at the buyer persona and demographic segmentation to determine personalised and best offers. A buyer persona is a portrayal of a single customer based on a group of customers and data. Demographic segmentation is best described as a conceptual group of customers based on certain specifics or geographical and cultural factors.

What to Do

To define the demographic segmentation of your target market focus on what is unique about your potential client. Find out if your market is local or global. Group together the collective data of your target client such as age, gender, status, family size, education, salary, languages spoken and location. The list goes on and on. Dig deep into the data, as there may be more applicable groupings for your business. This information will help you not only find your best market, but also to build and profile your buyer personas. You can promote and sell your products using a customary approach to a particular segment of your target market.

Tips and Take Homes

Don't stop at segmenting the buyer's profile; do the same for your market, product and industry. Explore other segmentations such as social, geographical and cultural groups. Use A/B product testing to analysis what market segments act best to your marketing and products.

Digital Nugget

Get your existing customers involved by using an online survey tool to get some quick results. Don't overload the survey with questions. Offer their name to be put into a draw to win a prize. This will encourage completion.

80. BECOME BIG ON THE LITTLE THINGS

How it Works

Little things make a big difference. It pays to become big on the little things when it comes to customer engagement. One of The City Bin Co.'s marketing themes is called *'Big on the Little Things.'* As a company we go the extra mile to make sure we get the job done. We make sure our trucks are spotlessly clean. We always leave the bins back where they were left and we make it easy for our customers to contact and talk to us.

In 2013, my wife and I bought a house in Alicante, Spain. I was amazed at the attention to detail from a small property auctioneer called *Inmobiliaria InmoXara*. They impressed me from the first contact, which happened online to the purchase of property and everything in-between. When we finally got the keys to our new home, Alex and Gemma from *Inmobiliaria InmoXara* presented us with a little box that read *'don't open until you are inside.'* The deal was already done. There was no need for them to be in the picture. When we got into our new home we opened the box. Inside there was a small bottle of champagne and two glasses with a note wishing us well. Why is this important? I haven't stopped telling people about them. By being big on the little things they have me telling everybody about my experience. Paddi Lund author of the book *'Building the Happiness-Centred Business'* refers to this as a *Critical Non-Essential*.

What to Do

Firstly, do the job right first and every time. See what value you can add in the process to complement the experience for the customer. Think about what happens after their buying transaction has ended and where you can genuinely wow them or be of assistance to them in any way. Look at what every business in your industry is doing and turn it on its head. Think of the extra little things you can do that you don't need to do but will set you apart.

Tips and Take Homes

Check out what is standard in other industries but not in yours. Brainstorm ways of introducing your findings. Being the first in your industry to do something will give the online and offline media a great reason to write about your business.

Digital Nugget

After the customer is finished with your service, touch base with them and ask for feedback via video. After my wife Eva purchased a wooden frame for growing vegetables in the garden from *Quickgrow*'s online shop, the company wowed her by not only delivering within 3 working days but by sending a follow-up leaflet with a gift and an offer of a free product if she sent on a video of her using their product.

81. USE WORD OF MOUTH MARKETING

How it Works

It's not what you do or say, it's what people see you doing or more to the point, see your customers doing that creates real word of mouth marketing. You, as a business, don't create word of mouth but you can actively guide the message and encourage it to spread when a positive story about your business is shining. Zappos, who never had a big advertising budget, credit its success story to word of mouth marketing. They focused on creating great customer experiences. Their end goal was to get their customers talking openly about their positive experience with Zappos. Tony Hsieh, CEO of Zappos.com said "Most of the money we would have spent on paid advertising or paid marketing we invest in customer service and the customer experience instead." Tony understood that the more loyal customers were the more the company would grow through word of mouth. In November 2009, Tony's customer centric word of mouth marketing paid off when Zappos.com was acquired by Amazon.com in a deal valued at $1.2 billion.

What to Do

Give your customers a great experience so that they will tell their friends about you and your business. Word of mouth starts with great customer service. Give your customers a reason to talk. Give them a reason to tell others to give your products a spin. Listen to what your customers are saying about their experience and perceptions of your product.

Tips and Take Homes

Wrap every interaction like it's out of a great story. Design and stage it until it's the done thing. It's human nature to want to share entertaining stories, so give them something positive and powerful to talk about. Wow your customers! Get people talking!

Digital Nugget

Social media has opened up a whole new world for word of mouth marketing. Promote your messages and good news stories to increase your reach and put your content in front of new potential clients. Make sure there is substance to the stories you are spreading. Keep them real.

82. MAXIMISE YOUR MARKETING SPACE

How it Works

Over the years I have seen so many missed opportunities to maximise on marketing when it comes to different types of paper and electronic communication with clients. From invoices, receipts and dockets to opening times and menus, you can now say much more to your customers. You can communicate about new products, give tips or inform them of community news.

What to Do

Map out all your paper and paperless interactions with you clients. See where you can use the space to say something interesting and share more information. For example, on your invoices you could have a space to insert a simple banner that promotes your different services. On The City Bin Co.'s commercial docket books we have an advert promoting our skip-hire service and on our invoices we notify our customers about our awards and charity of choice.

Tips and Take Homes

Make sure that the over-all purpose of the communication is well balanced and not crammed to the point where the customer is confused. In other words, an invoice is an invoice and is sent to customers for one reason: To get paid. Any other messages should not interfere with this and should be kept simple and subtle.

Digital Nugget

If your exchanges are done electronically, ensure the text or images are click-through enabled. Add links that guide the customer to a purchasing page or a video with more information on your products and news.

83. SUPPORT FESTIVALS, EVENTS AND INTERESTING SOCIAL PROJECTS

How it Works

When coordinators and promoters of festivals and events contact you looking for you to be a sponsor or offer your products or services for free, don't be too quick to say no. Festivals and events drive large volumes of people together to enjoy their time around a particular theme be it sailing, baking, food, arts, or simply beach cleaning and summer fun. Often the kneejerk response in business is 'well, you are damned if you do and you are damned if you don't.' This comes from fear of losing money to pay for the hype of somebody else's dream.

Many businesses say no because they look only at the financial cost. The goodwill is a term rarely valued. The value is in helping and if you can't help financially, find a way to do an exchange of goods. Give and receive. If you help out in some small way, you may gain from contributing.

What to Do

Never just say 'no'. Discuss first, when you get a request to offer your services for an event or festival, of course there is value. Of course there is a fee. As most events and festivals are done on a shoestring budget you will probably be asked for a donation or to provide services for free. I don't encourage doing anything for free but I do encourage getting involved in the events on some level. Exchange your services for billboard adverts in key locations. Trade your services for professionally taken photographs of your products in use. Where possible say yes, but ask the question:

'Before we commit what can you do for my business? How can you help me grow?'

If you know how your engagement with the footfall of the event can be beneficial, tell the organisers what you will need. When you commit to doing something with a project be sure to write up a press release and take some professional photos to send to the media. This way you gain maximum exposure for your company and the project in which you are involved.

Tips and Take Homes

It is impossible to do every event in your local town or city. Pick one or two that you feel you can create a meaningful partnership with and give support without becoming overloaded with pressure. It's about giving and helping.

Digital Nugget

Ask for photos and testimonials for your website. In 2014, when The City Bin Co. was asked to collect the bins for a popular charity fundraising event in the west of Ireland called *Bakefest,* we created a competition category called *'Bake it, don't bin it!'* and it was one of many categories. We asked the professional bakers at the event to bake cakes using our bins and logo as inspiration. The photos of the results were inspirational. People were baking our brand and the results went viral on social media. The winner was chosen from all the different categories, from wedding cakes to novelty cakes. The icing on the cake for our company was the overall winner was a cake based on our branding chosen from the category that we created. The upshot from this was that we received a lot of national publicity that we could never have anticipated before agreeing to help out at the event.

Document all these events by making small video diaries for your social media channels and to share with the event coordinators. Create a corporate social responsibility page on your website where you can document your involvement with such projects. Make sure there are links going back and forth from the webpages involved with your website. Most importantly, make it fun.

84. PR CRISIS MANAGEMENT: EXPECT THE UNEXPECTED

How it Works

PR crisis management means to expect and prepare for the unexpected and manage the unexpected to your advantage. When your marketing plan hits a wall, becomes entangled in a crisis or a competitor uses smear campaign tactics against your brand, you can be prepared.

What to Do

Don't panic. Do plan. When planning your marketing campaign anticipate all possible outcomes and design your response and desired results. This allows you to act and not react, which in turn keeps you in control of your desired destination should anything out of the ordinary happen. Always give absolute reassurance to your existing customers.

Identify 3 possible scenarios that constitute a crisis affecting your business. Based on these semi-fictional predictions design three emergency crisis management plans that will help you have the necessary response mechanisms in place. Establish a key response team within your business. Write pre-written press releases that reinforce your brand and commitment to provide the best customer service. Leave out the detail and dates. Include positive quotes from you emphasising the unity within your business and your focus on your customers. These will be on file and ready for use when needed. Select a spokesperson to implement the crisis management plan if and when needed. Pinpoint three media sources that you believe to be the best channels to communicate your message.

On the 27th of November 2012 The City Bin Co. opened a huge marketing campaign with digital, outdoor, print, TV and all possible outlets promoting our new service only to have 10 of our trucks burned out in an arson attack within 2 weeks. It was Friday night. Within 8 hours of the attack, Gene Browne, CEO of the company was on every Irish TV and radio channel and in the Irish newspapers with one simple message for existing customers and potential customers. The message was *'It's business as usual. Your bins will be collected and emptied as per usual first thing Monday.'* At the close of day the following Monday, we signed up over 2500 new customers.

We had already thought out what would happen if we got up one morning and none of our trucks worked. The proposed plan of action and the message was there. Give your customers reassurance that it's business as usual and follow through on that message.

Your objective is to know the impending trouble or the danger signals within your company and industry. Create an appropriate turnaround strategy to be in place in the event of a crisis. Crisis management is all about being prepared. Have an implementation plan in place for after a crisis that includes a change and monitoring process.

Tips and Take Homes

Brainstorm any eventualities that could cause a crisis within your company, your industry or your environment. Think about how your day-to-day trade and your business brand could be upset. Then draw up a plan of action to deal with such a crisis from the worst-case scenario to the best-case scenario. Study all past crises within your industry and the responses. If you are not sure where to start speak to a crisis management expert.

Digital Nugget

When there is a PR crisis, social media is where you will hear about it first and social media is where you need to respond. Use social media by paid advert campaigns to push out clear messages to speak to your customers in real time. Ask them to share your message. Be truthful, open and honest. Smoke and mirrors, dishonesty and secrecy only serve to prolong the crisis and sow doubt in customers' mind. If you are in the wrong put your hands up. Design clear messages to communicate with your customers online. Keep it professional and positive.

MASTER YOUR MARVELLOUS MARKETING SKILLS

There are a few basic marketing skills that can make a huge difference to your sales. Everybody involved in a business has a key role in marketing. All businesses are highly competitive. I can guarantee that your competitors are marketing very hard to keep you from the potential customer's door. To master your marketing skills, you need to think sales first and always. What is the end result you want to achieve with your marketing activity? Sales. How many new clients do you wish to bring on board? The answer is as many as you can handle. Brand awareness is great but it doesn't pay the bills. You have to take brand awareness one-step further and convert it to real sales. Meet with your fellow marketers and find out what is working for them. No business can afford to do marketing part time or to ignore it completely. If you have customers, marketing matters. If you have competition that are marketing their products and brand for your customers attention you must start marketing. Marketing is very multifaceted. You must develop and master a few of the essential skills if the results are to repay your efforts. Take time to learn new skills that better position you to engage with your customers and connect with potential prospects. Start networking to build contacts and tell your story to others. This is real relationship marketing. This is where you learn and pitch.

All marketing activities start with an idea. Don't lose the ideas. The good ones don't always come when you are sitting at your desk. Create one-page proposals of all your ideas. Put them down on paper. As Dermot McConkey, sales strategist once said at a Sales Master Minders meeting: *'Think with ink.'* Be a giver. Digital marketing tools and email make it really easy and cost effective to send a gift to your potential clients and customers. Send something such as a whitepaper or e-book. Get the experts talking about you and your brand.

Define what marketing is for you and make it work. Set targets and aim to reach them. Nobody else will do it for you. Don't forget about customers that you haven't heard from in a long time or have gone to a competitor. It's always good to touch base and re-ignite the old flames. If you don't know where to start, hook on to the hallmark days. Don't have brainstorms, have brain-dumps; more comes out! Add a lot of sex appeal. It has proven to work time and time again and most importantly: Never stop marketing.

85. DON'T TOOT YOUR OWN HORN!

How it Works

Blowing your own trumpet or talking about yourself is not a good idea when it comes to marketing. There is no flattery in self-flattery. Instead, get others talking about you. When Noel Kelly from Creva International is closing a new account he gives a gift of the Amazon bestseller *'The Binman's Guide to Selling'* to his new client with his interview page book marked. He does this for two reasons 1) to show gratitude to his client and 2) to demonstrate that the acknowledged experts are sharing his success story.

In Verne Harnish's latest best selling book *'Scaling Up'*, he speaks about The City Bin Co.'s methods of applying quarterly themes and employing staff who are focused on fitness. Verne's reason for writing about The City Bin Co. is because the company applied and executed the lessons from Verne's previous book *'The Rockefeller Habits.'* On occasion, I have tagged authors and blogged about experts who have influenced The City Bin Co. only to have them reply or comment on the blog. When David Meerman Scott, author of the *'The New Rules of Marketing & PR'* and *'The New Rules of Sales & Service'* (2 of my all-time favourite business books!) wrote about the social media success story of musician Amanda Palmer, it endorsed the unique drivers that make real time marketing work. It made his audience want to learn more. It told other creative individuals to look to Amanda for guidance. It added value to Amanda Palmer's brand. It made it more attractive to fans and patrons.

By obtaining endorsements from industry or business experts, you raise your profile and you gain credibility. This also keeps you at your best. You will work smarter to live up to the perception that has placed you in the spotlight. Art Turock, an elite performance provocateur, in the business leadership world cited The City Bin Co. for its leadership development process in his latest book titled *'Competent is Not an Option.'* Art once said, *'don't toot your own horn. Let a writer do it for you!'*

What to Do

First thing to do before any trumpets are blown is to get your house in order. Look for a great story that you have to tell. Look for the one thing you did that can help others. Who influenced you? Why were you successful? What template or revolutionary process did you follow? Blog about it and tell it on your social media.

Write the story. Invite movers and shakers in the business-influencing sphere to look at your amazing story. If there is a business expert, business journals or expert on a certain theme that resonates with your story, contact them. Send them an email. Meet them. Build a relationship with them. Involve them in your story and partake in any teachings or models they have created. Ask them how they would make your story better. Ask them to tell your story.

Tips and Take Homes

When you find the hook that is your story, keep it real and authentic. Do not create an imaginary story. Do not exaggerate the truth or lie. People connect with real people who tell real stories that touch them on an emotional level. They need to connect to your story by linking it to their own personal and current needs.

Digital Nugget

When you apply a technique or method to your business that is a success, connect with the creators of the process on all your online platforms. Become their poster boy company. Create a page on your website where you can invite others to tell your story.

86. MEET YOUR FELLOW MARKETERS

How it Works?

Every company in every industry is marketing in one form or another. Seek out the top marketing executives and hook up with them. Ask them for an hour of their time. Exchange stories. Learn what strategies worked for them and, just as important, what didn't work. Build relationships with them. If other experts in the marketing field know what you are doing, they will share ideas and lend a hand when you reach out. Build a community of fellow marketers. This is all about sharing ideas and trying out marketing methods from different industries. If you wish to be great at marketing and keep up to date with all the latest trends, surround yourself with the guys who are doing it right.

What to Do?

Research and choose five top marketers that you like across different industries. People that you believe can challenge you; individuals who have a proven track record. Write them a short e-mail to explain that you admire their work as a marketer and would like to do a video conference to learn more about what they do and how they do it. Reach out locally so that you can have face-to-face meetings with your marketing peers. Be up front and say why you wish to meet: to learn and to share marketing ideas that may be of benefit to all parties. Write out clearly what you want to learn before your get-together so that you can have successful meetings. Ask for advice and feedback. Give suggestions and brainstorm ideas. It can be of great value to receive expert insights from somebody who is not emotionally attached to your project or product.

Tips and Take Homes

Go to all possible networking groups in your area. Do this to meet contacts, but even more to learn effective communication skills such as listening, telling your story and building professional relationships.

Digital Nugget

When you have a collective of marketing peers, set up a private online group that will enable you to share ideas, successes and disappointments. This can act as a great real-time virtual adviser to your marketeering efforts.

87. NETWORKING: REAL RELATIONSHIP MARKETING

What to Do

Learn to network. Start networking. As humans, we are social by nature. That means doing more than connecting online. It means connecting on a one to one footing with the right people in the right environment. When I heard Sean Weafer, internationally renowned sales and networking expert, deliver a great talk at a Sales Master Minders event he spoke about the 2 reasons why people buy. Firstly, they buy on price and secondly, they buy on relationship. The potential client that will stay with you and pay top dollar for your product is the one that buys on relationship. Pursuing the perfect relationship with your potential clients starts and ends with the core of real relationship marketing, which is networking. As Sean summed it up so well at his talk: *"You can send an email, but you have no control over the opening of that email. When you network you are in control of building a solid relationship that can turn into sales and referrals down the road."*

How it Works

Join the local business communities, groups and chamber of commerce in you area. Make it your goal at each meeting to get 2 or 3 new contacts and meet them outside of the group for a coffee. This is where and how it starts. People that attend networking groups generally love to meet new people, so start by introducing yourself. Offer to meet up to learn more. Relationship marketing is about building personal relationships and a deeper understanding of the potential client so that when business is done it's done on the foundation that the relationship already exists.

Tips and Take Homes

If you are new to networking, always make the first move and introduce yourself. Learn who is in the room. If you don't get to talk one on one with everybody, follow up with an email and say:

'Sorry I didn't get a chance to say hello at the Sales Master Minders event. I would love to hear more about what you do. If you have 10 minutes for a quick coffee I would love to catch up.'

Digital Nugget

Link back your website to the website of the groups where you network to create useful links. Ask the groups to put a link for your website on their page. Let people know that you are open to networking by posting photos and blogs online. You can document notes about your networking sessions, which business people you met, what you learned and what you are going to implement from that meeting.

88. CREATE ONE PAGE MARKETING IDEA PROPOSALS

How it Works

The people who make marketing budget decisions may not prioritise your interests. I hold my hand up high in admitting that I have stormed into the CEO's office without an appointment and, with pure excitement, announced my brilliant light bulb idea. This approach normally doesn't go down too well. As a creative soul I found it hard not to express myself in the moment. I had to learn the hard way which, ultimately, works out to be an easier system with more chance of success. The best approach is to turn all ideas into one page marketing proposals. This way everything is documented. It is easy to present when the time is right. As a marketer, one of your jobs is to be creative and to be tuned into possibilities and opportunities that will help increase brand awareness and, more importantly, sales. Most ideas will make the chopping board with only a few being implemented. The ideas that don't make it may be parked because of timing, resources, lack of research or simply because they were not presented in the right light. When they are written up and saved you will have them for a later date.

What to Do

Create a simple template that can be used for every marketing idea or campaign that you believe is worth pursuing. This gives you a simple template to work from that can be documented, filed and stored. It also helps to have such a document when seeking others to come on board and back your idea. You can send them the one page marketing idea proposal in advance. Tailor the document to suit your business with an outline such as:

- Marketing campaign name
- Executive summary
- Objective and goals
- Target market research
- Estimated conversion rate
- Current position
- Costs
- Next step
- Price strategy
- Marketing outlets

- Sales strategy
- Estimated date of completion
- Timeline

When filling out these forms, keep them brief. If the idea can be expressed in a few lines, you can follow up with the detail later.

Tips and Take Homes

send a copy to your team. Ask them what they would change or do differently to make the idea better. This will encourage them to get involved in the marketing process of generating more creative concepts and produce more marketing ideas for the business.

Digital Nugget

Make your template available for your customers to download. Get them involved in your marketing planning using a crowd sourcing approach for your ideas.

89. GIVE A GREAT MARKETING ENCORE

How it Works

There is a wonderful feeling when you go to a music concert and see the crowd cheer and shout for an encore at the end. The band comes back on stage and delivers their best performance of the night. Everybody goes home wanting more. The great gigging bands are masters at this. They know how to play the crowd. Their timing is perfect. They deliver a great ending, hook the audience and seal the deal with a killer finish. Musicians are the greatest marketers of all time. They know how to bring you in, deliver an experience and top it off with an ace up their sleeve - a mindblowing little extra which surprises the audience and leaves them with the feelgood factor. On the 27th of November 2015, I flew a commercial Boeing 707 from Dubai to Hong Kong on iPilot, in the Dubai mall. iPilot is a flight simulator that is so authentic that even real pilots use it to train! The attention to detail and small gifts of a photograph and certificate after the flight made it an encore worth waiting for and repeating. I'll be back!

What to Do

Once your marketing plan is laid out and finalised, ask what is my encore? What could you do to give your potential clients and new customers that great feeling? What is that wow factor that your customers are not expecting but would leave them feeling good about the whole experience? When you welcome them into your brand club what community is there? What events can you create that your customers can enjoy collectively? What is the unexpected plus they will cheer and shout for? Map out the steps of your customer's journey from beginning to end. At the end, add a new step and call it the encore. Test out different experiences that will potentially be your encore.

Tips and Take Homes

When you find your encore, keep it a secret. By keeping the marketing encore a secret, it will be more of a surprise element when delivered.

Digital Nugget

Have one or two different micro-landing pages ready to go. These can be promoted on the digital landscape to let people know to spread the word about your marketing encore where applicable.

90. BE A GIVER

How it Works

When your potential client arrives on your website there are a few basics you want them to do. You want them to stay on your site for a while and look around. You want them to self-assess their needs for a purchase and you want them to feel good. The 'feelgood' buzz can be done with a simple exchange. It doesn't have to be anything that has a big cost to you. But it should definitely add value to their experience.

What to Do

Look at the homepage on your website and see where you can add a click-through banner that simply states 'Our gift to you.' The visitor to your website gives you their email address and you send them a gift. It's nice to touch base with a customer or potential customer once in a while, not to sell, but to send a gift that simply acknowledges the time they have spent checking out your products. It's a 'thank you.'

Tips and Take Homes

You could team up with a coffee shop and invite your customers to have a coffee on you! When people arrive at your website invite them to download a token they can print out and exchange at their local coffee shop.

Digital Nugget

An electronic gift of a PDF, whitepaper or booklet that shows them something useful, helps them solve a problem and makes life a little easier for them can go along way. For example, if you sell kitchen appliances and cookware, team up with a certified nutritionist and give a gift of the top ten tips from the top food expert brought to you by your brand.

91. RE-IGNITE YOUR OLD FLAMES

How it Works

You will win customers and you will lose customers. The automatic tendency is to look for new customers, which is logical in the sense that it seems easier to get them excited about your product. It is new to them after all. What is equally important, and often forgotten, is to spend some time romancing the old flames and winning back their affection for your brand.

What to Do

Create a winback campaign that is aimed at people who would have used your product at one stage or another and have left you for another brand or have simply no need for the product you sell. Touch base with them by inviting them back into your world. This is not for them to buy but for you to learn. Ask them why they aren't using your brand any more. Design a campaign inviting ex-users to tell you about their experience. This is important because if they stopped using your product because of price, quality or a bad customer experience, you give them the opportunity to be heard. You can hold your hands up and say: *'That was us then and this is us now and we would love for you to sample the new improved version.'* Ask them if they were to design your product what would it be like. This gives them an emotional involvement, which brings your brand onto their radar. Make it fun and remember, like the old flames that once captured your heart, if they don't want to go there that's okay too!

Tips and Take Homes

You are not going to win back every heart, however, there will be some ex clients that will give you another swing at the bat. You are not starting as an unknown. There is familiarity. Familiarity builds trust and this allows you to communicate and learn. Knowledge enables you to repackage, reposition and resell.

Digital Nugget

Test the water first by generating a small online winback campaign in the form of an adword campaign and an online survey with a small number of ex-clients. Use this to get an idea of how you will creatively construct your winback campaign.

92. LOOK FOR THE REAL TALENTS AND HOBBIES WITHIN YOUR BUSINESS

How it Works

When you know your employees' interests and talents, you can help them to help you in business. This bonding can build great teams within your business allowing for a healthy culture for people to work in. When your team knows you care about what drives them, they will help to push a little harder to drive your end goal. The result is higher productivity, focus and commitment. As the old phrase says: *'You scratch my back and I will scratch yours!'*

What to Do

Outside of the daily tasks and skills applied to make the business work, dig a little deeper and find out what the specific employees love to do and are good at doing outside of the workplace. What are their hobbies? You might be surprised to find that you have some champions and talent on your team that you never expected.

In September 2010, The City Bin Co. supported two employees who were budding songwriters to record and release a top 20 hit! One of whom was yours truly, and my brother Parisch Browne. All proceeds went to Hand in Hand Children's Cancer Charity, The City Bin Co.'s charity of choice at the time. We enlisted local singer, John Gaughan, to add the vocals. We came up with the idea while brainstorming ways to help the charity. We both enjoyed songwriting as a hobby and decided to go for the DIY option. We recorded a song on my eight track home studio. The song, titled 'That's What You Do', received local and national radio play reaching no 19 in Ireland's music charts keeping the international hit makers Black Eyed Peas at number 20. We raised a lot of publicity and money for the charity and the company got great media exposure.

At The City Bin Co., as well as chart topping musicans, we have had champion Irish dancers, world champion kickboxers, a county footballer, a national champion shooter and a world champion professional motorcycle streetbike freestyle rider to name a few. Every individual has a talent and hobbies within your business that you can support. The return for you is loyalty and a win for all parties involved.

Tips and Take Homes

Finding the connections between your staffs' hobbies, personal goals and the overall goal of the business can be difficult. Start finding the gems from within simply by asking. Invite your team to a brainstorming session where the real talent can be put on the table. Ask those with the skills or interest to drive projects with their skills and hobbies for mutual benefit.

Digital Nugget

The team building on such projects can be documented on a 'meet the team' style blog. When you come up with a plan, tie it all in with the company's sports and social club or charity so that you can also raise funds for a good cause. Allow your staff to contribute at every stage of this process.

93. REWARD, RECOGNISE AND SAY 'THANK YOU'

How it Works

An effective business loyalty program will encourage your top customers to return time and time again. It will provide you with the understanding needed to focus and win new customers. A great reward program gives gratitude and encourages the customers to talk about you. It enables you to up-sell and resell to your existing customers while building trust and rewarding loyalty.

What to Do

Identify your most loyal customers. Target them by offering a discount or an incentive. The idea of a reward system is to reinforce customer relations. This positive activity is strengthening your customer retention. Think about the incentives you are going to offer customers. You could create a club card that provides a discount with every purchase or a points system that lets your customers collect points and cash in on them or points that could be exchanged for a prize.

Tips and Take Homes

Don't reward all of your customers. Create a benchmark that your customers must reach to be rewarded. This creates competitiveness within the customer circle. Limit the rewards for certain periods enticing the customers to purchase product to gain more points.

Digital Nugget

Don't stop with the rewards. Reward, recognise and say 'thank you' by posting a picture of the client with a quote on a page dedicated to your most loyal clients. Issue digital certificates by email announcing the top clients that reach their targets and are rewarded.

94. DO IT ALL AT ONCE!

How it Works

Marketing campaigns have so many layers, from the latest geo-targeted digital advert campaigns to traditional outdoor poster promotions. It is important to give a balanced focus to each media channel that can genuinely have an impact on your sales. By restricting your campaigns to a particular channel, you miss opportunities to spread your message. Your potential customers are consuming more media through more channels than ever before. To reach and engage these people, you need to expand your marketing efforts across numerous touch points.

What to Do

Run your marketing campaign with a bang! Hit them from all angles! If your story or advert is on the radio when your potential clients tune-in, you also want the following: You want them to open the paper and see the visual version of your advert. You want them you switch on their PC and get the digital display version. When they are driving home you want them to see your adverts on billboards or on bus shelters. When they are watching their preferred TV program, you want them to see your brand in the commercial section. This is doing it all at once. They see it everywhere and you become recognisable more quickly. The more times people see it, the more comfortable they become with your brand. This is brand awareness. Getting your message out through many mediums at once creates brand familiarity and trust. These are two of the most important ingredients in bringing your potential customer closer to a purchase.

Tips and Take Homes

Keep the message consistent and to the point. Know why you need to say what you are saying. Is it to build brand awareness? Is it a direct call to action? Think about how you will measure the success of each strand of your marketing strategy.

Digital Nugget

Use your social media as a place to document all your adverts, media interactions and customer interactions. Use video and images to tell the campaign's story.

95. ASSOCIATE WITH A CELEBRITY!

How it Works

Known brands often invite celebrities to launch their products. You can do the same, linking with a person, event, place or day! Allow your business to be guilty by association. When I launched my first book, I invited Sean Gallagher to open the book launch. Sean is an experienced, international entrepreneur, speaker and a highly regarded business writer. By affiliating with Sean, I could link to a circle that was bigger and more influential than my own. On the night of the launch, Sean gave a dynamic speech on the topic of sales. His expertise in business proved beneficial to the success of the book through the great audience he gave me. With this affiliation, a friendship grew and Sean spoke at the inauguration of the successful Sales Master Minders business group, which I founded in 2014.

What to Do

Hire a celebrity, associate with a celebrity or become a celebrity! Start by creating partnerships and associations with everything you do. Everybody needs a team. Affiliate with others who have profile that can help move your products. It can be as simple as sponsorship, association with a famous individual or basically news jacking an event or, as I like to say: 'Hook onto a hallmark' day. The City Bin Co. love to market the hell out of Christmas and Valentine's Day, after all, their brand and product colour is red!

Tips and Take Homes

You are increasing your audience and tapping into a circle of influence other than your own. The main value here is that both you and your brand benefit from linking to another brand, person, event or day and that the other party may benefit also.

Digital Nugget

If you are teaming up with another brand, person or event, cross promote both parties on your online platforms and social media. Record pre-launch videos. Issue a press release and let the world know about your new connection.

96. HAVE A BRAIN DUMP

How it Works

All marketing starts with an idea. Not all ideas make it past the lips of the team members involved in dreaming up ideas while developing a marketing campaign. Normally, you would come up with 4 or 5 and throw all your energy behind what you believe to be the strongest idea. 'Brain Dumping' sessions is a terminology that I learned while participating in a Forth Innovation project facilitated by *Gijs Van Wulfen*, one of the world's leading experts in the field of innovation. It is an idea-generating tool that allows all involved to brain dump every possible idea good or bad that lingers in the back of their mind.

What to Do

Get a team together. Get brain dumping! This is the art of writing down every single idea or possibility that could be an option for your marketing campaign. Give yourself a target. You could have a session with 10 people. The objective could be to get as many ideas as possible in 10 minutes that would be great ideas for a marketing campaign. Use a whiteboard or post-its. This way others can see your ideas. This may trigger an idea for others. If everybody comes up with 10 ideas, you will have 100 ideas from which to find the magic marketing idea that will drive your campaign to increase sales. Have fun!

Tips and Take Homes

Best results will be achieved when done within the confines of a team that doesn't talk. Do it in silence. This allows for each idea to get seen without influence and without judgment.

Digital Nugget

This is more of an anti-digital nugget; however, it is important for the process. Switch off all phones, laptops, tablets and any other electrical devices that may be a distraction to the session. In fact when we had our sessions with Gijs we would switch off all our phones in place them in a box for the day!

97. ADD SEX APPEAL

How it Works

It's everywhere. Sex is used to sell in adverts now more than before. It's more open and more direct. It's not sex that sells; it's the sexuality and sex appeal that sells. When done right it works. When done wrong it can kill your marketing efforts and your reputation. It's about being tasteful, seductive and attractive without losing respect for your product or the people portrayed. Marketing campaigns have always used the 'sex sells' technique through visual mediums to sell their products. It works. Why does it work? It gets a reaction. It gets attention.

What to Do

Seduce your audience with sex appeal. Yes, sex still sells. If using soft sexual messages works for your product go for it. Test the water with a test audience if you are unsure. A hand with red nail polish touching your product can often do the trick. Be tactful and artistic. Keep it tasteful. Do not turn off any of your customers. The context is everything. Your goal is to draw your customer's attention in a positive way.

Tips and Take Homes

Always remember your product is the object and not the people portrayed. They are subjects with sex appeal who bring attention towards the object.

Digital Nugget

When you get the right tone, repeat it. Push it out on all your social media. Create a behind the scenes blog. Tell a story about why you designed your campaign with sex appeal. Bring your potential customers on the journey.

98. ALWAYS BE A SALES PERSON FIRST, MARKETER SECOND

How it Works

The role of marketing and selling is to grow revenue. Marketing and selling are so closely intertwined with each other that it can be next to impossible to see any difference. The same people in many businesses typically perform sales and marketing roles. Nevertheless, marketing is different from sales and as the business grows, the responsibilities become more specific to each role. The roles are always touching each other. When you know the potential client that you are selling to, you can design a better message for your target market. The best way to learn how to market is to learn how to sell first. For me it all started on the back of the truck. After my first few years on the front line, I moved into the office to answer phones and fold letters. I then went to work in the product delivery division and progressed to commercial sales where I worked for almost 10 years. After that I made the transition from sales to marketing. This is where I realised that my experience from the back of the truck to the heart of the sales team was the best training I could ever have received for my role on the marketing team for The City Bin Co. I had learned to communicate with the customers. I had learned to listen to the customers and, through my role in sales, I learnt to pay attention to the conversion of sales through the different channels of marketing.

What to Do

Before diving straight into your marketing strategy and implementation, spend some time with the sales team. Don't just follow them on their day-to-day routine. Join them. Be part of their team. Go out and meet the potential clients. Go door-to-door. Sign them up. Get them over the line. Discover what works and what does not work. Listen to the language used by the clients.

Tips and Take Homes

The more marketing you do the less selling you need to do to win potential customers. But, this is only true where the marketing efforts implemented are targeted and accurate. The best place to learn the tools to achieve this is out in the field selling.

Only when your selling becomes a simple transactional process that is clocking in the numbers will you be able to say that your marketing is working. With this in mind, design your offering so it is just that: a transactional process.

Digital Nugget

From what you learn with your sales hat on, generate word-clouds of the language spoken by the customers that you can reuse in your marketing campaigns when communicating with your potential clients.

99. MASTER YOUR MINDFULNESS FOR SUCCESSFUL MARKETING

How it Works

To have success in marketing you have to work at becoming more mindful. Then, you can tackle the marketing. It is always good to stand back from the madness of it all and bring silence to the mind. To master what you receive externally you need first to master the mind internally. To be of service to others you must first be of service to yourself. You need to become the best possible version of yourself. To do this you need to focus on three aspects of you life. They are:

- Health
- Family and friends
- Personal growth

Your health is your wealth. Like a plant, if your body doesn't get the right amount of sun or the right amount of water it may struggle to grow or to be strong. Your family and friends are very much part of your life story and it is important to check in and nourish these relationships.

Look after the nest, feed the family and have fun. This is why you do what you do. Don't lose yourself in the world of business at the expense of loved ones. Let great quality relationships drive you to succeed in business. Personal growth happens when you step outside your comfort zone and allow for new experiences.

There is so much noise in business and marketing from emails to cold calls, adverts and leaflets all trying to out sell, out gloss and out do one another. You don't have to be one more loud voice that can't be heard.

The best thing you can do is stop. Stop focusing on your job, tasks, campaigns and goals. You don't always have to run with the herd. Stop so you can rest. Stop so you can restart from a better place. Rest equals strength. Building your inner-strength is the secret for success. Master your marketing mindfulness by taken time out. This is the most powerful step in hitting the bull's-eye and collecting the gold. Most great athletes will stop and rest before competing. It gets the mind fresh and focused for the task ahead. Try it!

What to Do

For optimum health, exercise the body and the mind. To exercise, take thirty minutes, 3 times a week or every second day. Do physical activity. Go for a walk. Go for a run or a swim. Relax and recharge. This is very productive and is where you will get some of your best business ideas. To exercise your mind take thirty minutes on the days you are not exercising and meditate. Just sit and breathe and focus on your breathing and nothing else for that short time. **You have to switch off to switch on**. It seems mad; but it is true. Look at your food and what you eat. If you are not sure where to start ask an expert. Make a decision not to eat too much junk food. Eat the right food and drink lots of water. This is your fuel. Clare Rooney, personal trainer and nutritional expert, once put it perfectly to me, when she said, *'You wouldn't put diesel into a car that needed petrol!'* Of course not! And if you did you would feel a little silly, fix the situation and not do it again.

Healthy relationships with family and friends are important for a balanced mindset. Spend time with people you love. Let every Sunday be family and friends day. Get out of the house and have fun. Don't let anything take this away from you. This is like pouring buckets of happiness over your head. Don't talk work. Talk dreams. Talk rubbish. Tell stories. Do new things – Go and dance, sing, see a movie, cook a meal, start a new activity and meet new people. Let your hair down. This is living. This is being creative. This is when the best ideas come. They come when you are not forcing a thought and not thinking hard on a project. They come when you are relaxed and enjoying life.

Personal growth is bettering yourself and your personal skills through learning life lessons with new experiences. You must grow to learn and learn to grow. Success happens for those who master mindfulness in their business. Getting mentored and being a mentor is a great way to give and receive personal growth. With the right mentor there is great insight, ideas, goal setting and accountability. In mentoring there is a great satisfaction in helping someone see the light and seeing them succeed.

Tips and Take Homes

Rate your health, family, friends, fun and personal growth weekly. If you find that you rate one at 50 percent or less ask yourself what do you need to do to get to your desired rating. What do you need to stop doing? Or what do you need to start doing?

Over time you will be able to see patterns in your ratings. This will help you focus on where you need to improve. This is a great benchmark for your work-life balance. When you rate these pillars consistently high and they are all going extremely well you will have mastered mindfulness. This will position you to have your better marketing results in business.

Digital Nugget

Do a digital detox! Marketers generally tend to be glued to some type of electronic device twenty-four hours a day and seven days a week. Pick a day that you can switch everything off. Go 'old school' for a day and see what amazing ideas pour out of your creative mind. Despite what I've preached throughout this book, when you switch off the world of technology you will not miss a thing. You will have a new sense of energy and a pair of fresh eyes on your business and marketing campaign when you get back online.

100. NEVER STOP MARKETING!

How it Works

The more you bring marketing into your daily business activities the better you become at learning who your customers are. You become better at attracting and bridging the gap between customers who are simply looking and those who are buying. Marketing is for every business size. When marketing sits at the core of every one of your activities, you will find your sales going up. The purpose of marketing is to drive and support sales.

What to Do

When your marketing efforts bring in your first few customers you will want to focus all your time on delivery. This doesn't mean the marketing needs to stop. If the marketing stops, the leads will dry up. If you are unsure where to start so that marketing flows use the calendar year: The New Year marketing campaign, followed by a Valentine's campaign, followed by summer sale, followed by a back to school campaign, then a Halloween campaign, and finally a Christmas campaign! Never think budget, think project. Have a few projects lined up ahead of time so when the timeline for one project is coming to an end you can be preparing for the next.

Tips and Take Homes

Never let a campaign end and do nothing. Link one campaign after another. Your budget may go up and down but never stop marketing. Marketing, when done correctly generates leads. The leads are sales waiting for conversion. Never break the flow. Always document your campaign results so that you can improve on each campaign.

Digital Nugget

It's the very same online. Keep your online campaigns going and allow for overlapping. While one campaign is winding down use promoted soft advert campaigns to give a hint of the next project before it has even formally started.

MEET THE MARKETING LEADERS

Imagine having the opportunity to listen to the secrets of 50 of the world's top marketing executives. Imagine if you could tap into their great business minds. Imagine asking them for advice on what you should be focusing on and talking to them about what they do most when they have their marketing hat on. That is exactly what you will have as you read over this, the last and most important chapter in the book. You will have a moment with each and every one of them. If you were to meet them in real life and have that moment, I am sure you would put into practice any advice or tips that they would share with you. You would want to improve your marketing skills and especially when their words of wisdom could lead to increased sales. The people sharing the information have a proven track record of doing it smart. They get great results that bring in the sales. After all, we all market to sell. Learn how the best of the best in marketing understand the importance of measuring everything. They set objectives. They research and plan. They select relevant KPI's. They understand that these numbers are key to making decisions that will drive sales. You can turn *'I think that we are doing great'* into *'I know we are doing great'* when you have the data to back it up. Learn about the structure that the top marketers place on their marketing campaigns. Apply them to your operations. Make sure there is clarity around your objectives. Keep your sales team and your management team briefed on all details of the campaigns. This creates a healthy culture and a great source of frontline information adding strength to your marketing efforts. Experiment with your creativity. Try new things. Investigate new channels. Test the market. Measure its impact. Get out and speak to your existing customers. Listen to your customers. Ask them about the challenges that they face. Listen to the language they use. Spend time on product improvement. Keep asking yourself *'How can I be of service?'* and *'How can I improve what I already deliver?'* Study other businesses in other industries. Find out what is unique and works in other industries. Think about how you can cross over your learnings successfully to your business. I did the following interviews using every type of communication including face-to-face, phone calls, emails, Skype calls and Apple's face-time! I made a lot of notes and highlighted the parts that resonated with me. I encourage you to do the same. This is an opportunity for you to get new ideas and new skills. Use this knowledge with your own marketing practices. These pages are about to plug you into the best in marketing. Take it, use it and see your marketing strategy increase your sales in no time.

Meet Eventbrite
Marino Fresch | Head of Marketing | UK & Ireland

Eventbrite is a self-service ticketing website and live experiences marketplace. Eventbrite started in 2006, they have processed over 200 million tickets for events in more than 180 countries, and several thousands of event organisers use the platform every month.

Question 1: *What are your top marketing words?*

ROI, content, relevance, personas, net promoter score, customer lifetime value, and the *Pareto* principle.

Question 2: *What are the key ingredients for a successful marketing campaign?*

Providing a benefit is good, but solving a pain point is better. Focus on what you can **measure** and optimise relentlessly.

Question 3: *What is your top tip for marketing?*

In reality, marketing success rarely comes from a single *aha* moment, but instead 100 or 1000 small things that build over time. The most effective route to marketing success is to test many things, fail fast, and learn quickly.

Question 4: *What's your advice to somebody starting a career in marketing?*

Marketing is a really broad discipline. Figure out what aspect of marketing appeals most to you, and learn everything you can get your hands on about it. Companies want to hire specialists.

Question 5: *What do you spend most of your time doing when you have your marketing hat on?*

I spend a lot of time looking at the data, to understand what is working and what isn't. I'm always looking for new channels to test and for parts of my customer funnel that I can optimise.

Meet Paddy Power
Cormac Folan | Social Media Advertising Manager | Ireland

Paddy Power is an Irish bookmaker well known for its clever and successful online marketing. Cormac manages a multi-million euro budget across Facebook and Twitter focusing on driving new customer acquisition, promoting the Paddy Power brand and increasing the value of existing customers.

Question 1: *What are your top marketing words?*

Know your **customer** and know your **tone of voice** for communicating with them. Have specific goals for all campaigns and ensure that you look at the right **metrics** for measuring them, looking at a fully attributed view of each marketing channel based on their purpose.

Question 2: *What are the key ingredients for a successful marketing campaign?*

Clear KPIs are vital, understanding exactly what success looks like and what metrics to use to measure the campaign. A well-planned and executed campaign will be consistent across all platforms with the right creative imagery for each platform.

Question 3: *What is your top tip for marketing?*

Stay on top of all the latest trends and updates on all marketing platforms. Digital marketing is evolving rapidly and if you don't stay up to date it is very possible you will not be getting the most out of your campaign.

Question 4: *What's your advice to somebody starting a career in marketing?*

Learn how to use excel and **make decisions on data, not on opinion**. Test everything, all the time.

Question 5: *What do you spend most of your time doing when you have your marketing hat on?*

Working with my team and management to develop our strategy and build campaigns based on constant testing and learning. Looking at the full view of the campaigns we run and trying to measure the ROI of our spend.

Meet The City Bin Co.
Cosmin Gliga | Business Deelopment Manager | Ireland

The City Bin Co. is an industry leader when it comes to marketing, PR and online communication. The company has been winner of the Deloitte Best Managed Companies (Ireland) Award 2009, 2010, 2011 & Gold Standard Winner 2012. The City Bin Co. became the European Business Awards National Champions in Customer Focus in 2013.

Question 1: *What are your top marketing words?*

- Customers and communication
- Metrics and media
- Selling and service

Question 2: *What are the key ingredients for a successful marketing campaign?*

Get the right team together. Plan the campaign well in advance. Design it around a strong message. Don't be afraid to test new things, you could be surprised. Measure your marketing success. If it is not working: scrap it and re-start.

Question 3: *What is your top tip for marketing?*

Spend time researching your target market. Know your potential customers and know why they would engage with you. Do this by communicating with your current customers.

Question 4: *What's your advice to somebody starting a career in marketing?*

Find out who is doing marketing right and learn from them. Observe their greatness and their weakness. Look outside your own industry for these influences. Then, learn by doing.

Question 5: *What do you spend most of your time doing when you have your marketing hat on?*

Communicating with the customer. Looking for ways to continuously improve the experience that we deliver.

Meet Ryanair
Peter Bellow | Head of Sales and Marketing | Ireland

Peter, a 30-year veteran of the airline, airport and tourism industry has been involved in start-ups and multi nationals. Peter was the new head of sales and marketing which completely changed the customer proposition and created the companies' first pan European integrated TV, press and digital campaign.

Question 1: *What are your top marketing words?*

Profit, simplicity, consistency, integration, clarity and maintaining the same message for the group across 29 countries. Reinforce the indicators of success. Cost control. Load factor. Punctuality. Share price. Growth story.

Question 2: *What are the key ingredients for a successful marketing campaign?*

If you can measure it effectively – then you can manage it.

Question 3: *What is your top tip for marketing?*

Never forget the importance of old fashioned techniques such as use of earned media/PR and simple but mobile adaptive emails. Email is still the killer digital application.

Question 4: *What's your advice to somebody starting a career in marketing?*

Don't start in marketing. Start in sales first. If you can learn how to sell face to face or over the phone to someone successfully – then a classical marketing approach will seem easy and you will be more results orientated.

Question 5: *What do you spend most of your time doing when you have your marketing hat on?*

Finding ways in the traditional media to generate column inches, TV time and radio minutes.

Meet BNI
Dr. Ivan Misner | Founder & Chairman | U.S.A.

Dr. Ivan Misner is the Founder & Chairman of BNI, the world's largest business networking organization. BNI was founded in 1985. The organization now has over 6,500 chapters throughout every populated continent of the world. In 2013 alone, BNI generated 5.4 million referrals resulting in over $6.5 billion US dollars' worth of business for its members.

Question 1: *What are your top marketing words?*

Start learning about referral marketing and networking as a marketing tool. You may not have a global business but you can have a global reach. You can be a local business with a worldwide network. It's all about relationship building that go both wide and deep.

Question 2: *What are the key ingredients for a successful marketing campaign?*

A marketing campaign has to resonate with your target market or it becomes irrelevant. Use online networking to makes a difference. Technology has flattened the communication hierarchy. Understand that this enables you, in a digital marketing campaign to connect with all potential clients globally.

Question 3: *What is your top tip for marketing?*

Engage with your customers and all relevant parties involved. Culture eats strategy for breakfast, so get the company culture right before embarking on a marketing campaign.

Question 4: *What's your advice to somebody starting a career in marketing?*

Seek out additional training on selling. Learn about networking and referral marketing. The best way to do this is practice.

Question 5: *What do you spend most of your time doing when you have your marketing hat on?*

I focus on brand building using education, interviews and communication.

Meet MicksGarage.com
John Smyth | Senior Marketing Executive | UK & Ireland

John has been at the forefront of the mechanics that has seen the MicksGarage.com brand grow to become one of the largest car parts and accessories online retailers in the UK & Ireland. They deliver products to over 70 countries worldwide.

Question 1: *What are your top Marketing words?*

Target, expression, message, incentive, customer, creative, value, content, brand, and measure.

Question 2: *What are the key ingredients for a successful marketing campaign?*

Do your research. Know your audience. Know what they expect and where they consume their media. Put a plan and structure in place, including a full roll out plan and expected outcomes. Be creative and think outside the box - do something different that your competitors have never done.

Question 3: *What is your top tip for marketing?*

Go beyond your pure marketing activity. Where do users go to next, be it your shop or website. What do they expect to see? Is your message brought across and do you do what you say you do.

Question 4: *What's your advice to somebody starting a career in marketing?*

Think digital, it's not going away! Think mobile; everybody has one. It's growing. Internet and download speeds are getting better.

Question 5: *What do you spend most of your time doing when you have your marketing hat on?*

I first put myself in the shoes of the person who will be on the receiving end of it and try and get a feel for how they would react to it. If you approach any marketing activity only thinking of you as the company then you're going to miss a vital element of the message, which the user must grasp, understand and react to easily.

Meet Stocktaking.ie
Patrick McDermott | Managing Director | Ireland

Patrick has build Stocktaking.ie into an award winning national business that employs over 40 people. They provide an outsourced stocktaking service where the focus is on the accuracy of stocktaking. His clients include retail, pharmacy and hospitality.

Question 1: *What are your top marketing words?*

- **You**: Marketing is about tailoring your business message and values around your customer and not about yourself. Don't forget this.
- **Value**: Marketing is communicating the value that your business provides more than the customer pays. The customer is getting something rather than losing something.
- **Hassle-Free**: Make your service easy to understand and use.
- **Clarity**: Your message must be clear and easy to understand.
- **Solution**: Your customer has a problem, your business has the solution. Easy decision for the customer to choose your business.

Question 2: *What are the key ingredients for a successful marketing campaign?*

A successful campaign is not about one thing, its a combination of events to remind/reinforce the messages that have being portrayed to date. A clear message for your product/service which solves a problem that your target market has.

Question 3: *What is your top tip for marketing?*

Think of who you are marketing to and what they require. Be specific and tailor your marketing campaign accordingly. Make it memorable/sticky. Have a theme to your messages so as to make your brand recognisable and memorable. Bargain and haggle so as your money is spent wisely and goes as far as possible. Regularly follow up and meet to see if you can get more value from your campaign. Remember, your marketing should lead to sales, so ensure that you use metrics for measuring the effectiveness of your campaign.

Question 4: *What's your advice to somebody starting a career in marketing?*

It was said to me many years ago, *'Sales people make you money, marketing people spend your money'*. With this in mind, those embarking on a career in marketing MUST add value to their clients. Take time to understand their business and focus on their customer wants and needs. Tailor the marketing message accordingly. If you do this then you will have a repeat customer.

Question 5: *What do you spend most of your time doing when you have your marketing hat on?*

I act as if I am my target customer. I look at what I would want from a stocktaking company. Talking to others to see if my initial idea can be strengthened or if they have other ideas to add. I look for new ways to get in front of my target market. This can be in the form of writing articles for trade magazines, forming partnerships with other businesses who serve the same customers but are non-competing or joining trade organisations/representative bodies who represent my customers. These are excellent ways of getting introductions, referrals, and face time with potential customers.

Meet Microsoft
Zeid Shubailat | Marketing Lead | Middle East and North Africa

Zeid worked on IT transformation projects with a number for Fortune 100 companies, established Public Private Partnerships between Microsoft and Governments, and is currently responsible for the transformation journey of the North Africa, Eastern Mediterranean, and Pakistan subsidiary. Microsoft started with a mission of having a computer on every desk in every home and, more recently, the company wants to enable people and businesses throughout the world to reach its full potential through the use of software.

Question 1: *What are your top marketing words?*

Customer insight, targeting/segmentation, communication channels and ROMI (Return on Marketing Investment).

Question 2: *What are the key ingredients for a successful marketing campaign?*

Have a clear value proposition, targeting the right audience, with the right message, at the right time. Then follow it.

Question 3: *What is your top tip for marketing?*

Marketing is about knowledge of the market. The more you know, the better decisions you can make.

Question 4: *What's your advice to somebody starting a career in marketing?*

Ensure that you believe in the product and company you are going to market. You won't be passionate about the product unless you believe in it.

Question 5: *What do you spend most of your time doing when you have your marketing hat on?*

Analysing and increasing market knowledge is the external top of mind. Evaluating what team capabilities we need for success is the main internal focus.

Meet OnePageCRM
Michael FitzGerald | CEO and Founder | Ireland

Michael FitzGerald's OnePageCRM is a platform that provides an easy but powerful sales application for small business. It converts leads to customers fast on a simple dashboard, and does it with a beautiful user experience.

Question 1: *What are your top marketing words?*

- **Story**: Especially for startups - people and early adopters of your product are as much interested in your story.
- **Cadence**: Marketing is about 'showing up' for the small jobs every day, everywhere.
- **Consistency**: If you are to grow your brand, you need to start sounding "boring to yourself" but not necessarily your market.
- **Alive**: Emanate life from your organisation. People will judge you on whether they think you are current and in vogue.

Question 2: *What are the key ingredients for a successful marketing campaign?*

Finding the USP for that market segment and making sure it resonates. The rest of it is then easier.

Question 3: *What is your top tip for marketing?*

Stop thinking about your brand as a logo and think of it as every touch point in your organisation. From the product to it's packaging, your support centre to your social media comments. Everywhere.

Question 4: *What's your advice to somebody starting a career in marketing?*

You need to get comfortable with analytics and reading the metrics that are available to the modern marketer.

Question 5: *What do you spend most of your time doing when you have your marketing hat on?*

What will make us 'remarkable'; I focus on having a great product that is spoken about and recommended.

Meet Sharkey Consultants
Dr. Ultan Sharkey | CEO | Ireland

Dr. Ultan Sharkey is an E-commerce consultant specialising in online retail shopping and an adjunct lecturer in Business Information Systems at the National University of Ireland in Galway. He develops and implements corporate online strategies for online retail, booking, and subscription based services. With clients in Australia, South America, Canada, the United States, UK and Ireland, Sharkey Consulting continues to help companies refocus their online efforts for maximum performance.

Question 1: *What are your top marketing words?*

With so much competition for marketing keyphrases, our marketing strategy has been to leverage our competencies in specific ecommerce software packages such as Joomla, Magento, and Wordpress by marketing our practical skills in realising online strategies with these systems. That allows us to show our strengths and market in a niche way, without getting lost in the crowd.

Question 2: *What are the key ingredients for a successful marketing campaign?*

To me, marketing is a continuous learning about your customers. I enjoy tracking the process, campaign progress and results before tweaking my efforts and doing it all again. I firmly believe that without tracking and tweaking we are just swinging in the dark. Philadelphia department store giant John Wannamaker is thought to have said that half of his marketing efforts were wasted - he just didn't know which half. We have no such woes in modern marketing.

Question 3: *What is your top tip for marketing?*

Connect the dots. When you are correctly tracking your marketing efforts and spend for a time you begin to see the patterns emerge. Knowing your average conversion rate across your media allows you to easily say yes or no to a specific spend because you can predict the likely sales outcome. Knowing how your outcomes feed back to your campaign creation makes it a game-like process that you can continuously succeed at.

Question 4: *What's your advice to somebody starting a career in marketing?*

There is so much information out there purporting to be the next big thing or the best way to do this and that - the best advice I can give is to train yourself to filter and weigh what you learn. Business decision making has become increasingly strengthened by the scientific approach since Taylor's work in 1880s manufacturing. Putting your trust in the information you receive means developing the ability to identify high calibre knowledge.

Question 5: *What do you spend most of your time doing when you have your marketing hat on?*

Getting inside the mind of the client. I have plenty of experience creating and tracking marketing campaigns; the back-end of it all is second nature to me by now. Most of my marketing time is now spent trying to understand how my clients seek my services, and identifying ways in which I can engage with them where they are most comfortable.

Meet Digital Marketing Institute
Anthony Quigley | CEO | Ireland

Anthony Quigley is a leading digital marketer and expert in all things digital. As the founder and CEO of the Digital Marketing Institute, Anthony is considered one of the pioneers of digital marketing in Ireland.

Question 1: *What are your top marketing words?*

Top marketing words start with the customer! Traditional marketing was focused on the shotgun approach – i.e. throw enough mud and some of it will stick. This approach is way out of date. Using digital tools, you can not only target your customers but you can also measure the success on marketing campaigns.

Question 2: *What are the key ingredients for a successful marketing campaign?*

Start with the customer and work back from there. Successful marketing campaigns are focused on the customer.

Question 3: *What is your top tip for marketing?*

Be clear about what you want to say to the target sector and make sure that your marketing is finely segmented. Understand the difference between the target sectors, what they require and what makes them different.

Question 4: *What's your advice to somebody starting a career in marketing?*

Understand digital. Digital marketing is driving all innovation in marketing. Get to know all aspects of digital. If you want to succeed in marketing, you absolutely must know about the digital space.

Question 5: *What do you spend most of your time doing when you have your marketing hat on?*

I spend most of my marketing time thinking about the customer - what do they look like, what do they like, would they like what I am selling, how they want to be sold to and what form of communication do they prefer? Most marketing mistakes are made by not thinking like the customer. Get into their shoes, stand there and be that customer.

Meet The Bold Choice
Jane Rodriguez del Tronco | CEO | Spain

With a background in marketing for multi-nationals, Jane uses her marketing skills in talent development. She runs Spain's leading training and executive coaching company.

Question 1: *What are your top marketing words?*

- Coaching
- Talent
- Leadership
- Value
- Success
- Passion

Question 2: *What are the key ingredients for a successful marketing campaign?*

Keep it simple, focused and with an element of surprise. **Engage your clients**!

Question 3: *What is your top tip for marketing?*

Listen to your customers first! It's all about them, about what they need and what they love.

Question 4: *What's your advice to somebody starting a career in marketing?*

Go where your clients / customers go. Try to experience what they experience, to feel what they feel... and you will know how to surprise and engage them with your brand!

Question 5: *What do you spend most of your time doing when you have your marketing hat on?*

Making sure that our marketing plan, our activities, either offline or online, are supporting our position and driving us to achieve our goals.

Meet TheDocCheck.com
Dr. Niall McElwee | CEO | Ireland

After fifteen years a senior academic Niall set up his own company in 2009 where he is senior editor and Managing Director of TheDocCheck.com, a bespoke academic mentoring, editing and full writing solutions service for third level students and the SME business community.

Question 1: *What are your top marketing words?*

- Honesty
- Fluency
- Reach
- Targets
- Measurable
- Outcomes

Question 2: *What are the key ingredients for a successful marketing campaign?*

There must be measurable results that exceed the expectation of the client.

Question 3: *What is your top tip for marketing?*

Be courageous in your approach and be different to your competitors.

Question 4: *What's your advice to somebody starting a career in marketing?*

Study very carefully your market and always attempt to be more innovative than your peers. What might not work on a Monday may well change by Friday. Trust your intuition when you think you have a good idea.

Question 5: *What do you spend most of your time doing when you have your marketing hat on?*

I attempt to come up with strategies and campaigns that are innovative, fresh and interesting for my own team as well as our clients. I tend to research very diverse sources from around the world to see what works.

Meet Charlie Byrne's Bookshop
Olivia Lally | Marketing Manager | Ireland

Olivia looks after the online communication for Charlie Byrne's bookshop, one of Ireland's best-loved independent bookshops. Known as a browser's paradise in the book world, Charlie Byrne's bookshop was named Irish Times Best Bookshop in Ireland.

Question 1: *What are your top marketing words?*

- Passion
- Enthusiasm
- Value

Question 2: *What are the key ingredients for a successful marketing campaign?*

We always combine genuine passion for books with great value.

Question 3: *What is your top tip for marketing?*

Only share things you really care about – real passion and quality market themselves.

Question 4: *What's your advice to somebody starting a career in marketing?*

Marketing is a 24/7 job, that takes passion and commitment, so it's important to work on projects that inspire you with genuine enthusiasm for a product or service.

Question 5: *What do you spend most of your time doing when you have your marketing hat on?*

We are very active on social media, and enjoy connecting with our customers through Facebook, Twitter and Pinterest. We also have a very active website, which is used primarily to share our passion for books and love for literature, rather than as an ecommerce tool. This helps build a relationship with customers, and allows visitors experience Charlie Byrne's virtually. Recently, we've been nominated for several awards, and work hard to promote these, and use them to attract new customers and promote the shop image internationally.

Meet Tayto
Elly Hunter | Marketing Brand Manager | Ireland & UK

As the Marketing Director for the Tayto brand for the past 6 years, Elly is charged with maintaining market leadership and consumer love! She delivers this through innovative new product and flavour launches, promotions, PR and local marketing.

Question 1: *What are your top marketing words?*

- Iconic
- Love
- Passion
- Loyalty
- Trust
- Tayto!

Question 2: *What are the key ingredients for a successful marketing campaign?*

Consumer attraction and consumer buy-in.

Question 3: *What is your top tip for marketing?*

Trust in your own gut feel, research and fact based insight take time and money. FMCG (Fast moving consumer goods) marketing needs to be fast paced and on the seat of the pants!

Question 4: *What's your advice to somebody starting a career in marketing?*

Listen, look and learn. Experience comes from moving jobs every few years. Everyone is an expert in marketing but only those with experience and confidence to make instant decisions and to say no progress

Question 5: *What do you spend most of your time doing when you have your marketing hat on?*

Multi-tasking!

Meet CoderDojo
Bill Liao | Founder | Ireland

Bill Liao is Co-Founder of WeForest.org and CoderDojo.com, the famous worldwide movement that gets kids into programming computers so they become native digital creators.

Question 1: *What are your top marketing words?*

- Poets
- Coder
- Dojo
- Magic
- Power
- Smiles

Question 2: *What are the key ingredients for a successful marketing campaign?*

- Crispness
- counterintuitivity
- story
- denouement
- surprise
- satisfaction

Question 3: *What is your top tip for marketing?*

Test and measure the hell out of every message in an objective way until every sound bite shines. Market the happy people your organization has pleased. Never talk about your technology.

Question 4: What's your advice to somebody starting a career in marketing?

Go into PR or become really really good at math.

Question 5: *What do you spend most of your time doing when you have your marketing hat on?*

Testing and spreading memes.

Meet Tree Light Pictures
Josef Hrehorow | Managing Director | Ireland

Josef has led Tree Light Pictures to be one of Europes leading coporate video making companies. They creates unique, high production value video content exclusively for businesses and brands. To date they have worked with brands such as Intel, Red Bull and Primark. As a team they have worked in locations as diverse as Burkina Faso, Uganda and multiple locations across Europe and USA. In the summer of 2013 they created the viral video content for Coláiste Lurgan which exceeded 10 million views and featured on television worldwide.

Question 1: *What are your top marketing words?*

- Content
- Value
- Openness
- Goals
- Targets

Question 2: *What are the key ingredients for a successful marketing campaign?*

Consistency & creativity.

Question 3: What is your top tip for marketing?

Find out where you're wasting your time early and then move on.

Question 4: *What's your advice to somebody starting a career in marketing?*

List what you don't know and commit to finding the answers. Identify the high quality experts early and follow them. Be picky on who you choose to listen to, You don't have the time to listen to poor quality experts.

Question 5: *What do you spend most of your time doing when you have your marketing hat on?*

Thinking of content that we can create and share with our fans. Written blogs, vlogs, video series, ebooks, infographics etc.

Meet DoneDeal.ie
Agnes Swaby | Marketing Manager | Ireland

Agnes Swaby looks after the marketing for Ireland's most successful classified adverts website: *Donedeal.ie* - The Business claims a market leadership position four times as big as its nearest competitor. The company provides an easy safe marketplace for people to buy or sell all sorts of things. Founded in 2005, the business has steadily grown and claims up to 500,000 visitors to its website each day. On average, 140,000 new items are advertised each month. The site currently has over 230,000 adverts active on the website.

Question 1: *What are your top marketing words?*

- Top of mind
- Brand awareness
- PR
- Sponsorship

Question 2: *What are the key ingredients for a successful marketing campaign?*

Ensure you use a 360 approach and that you are hitting the right audience at the right time.

Question 3: *What is your top tip for marketing?*

Do **research** prior to a campaign and post campaign.

Question 4: *What's your advice to somebody starting a career in marketing?*

Do not take a sales job, hold out for a marketing role - something will turn up.

Question 5: *What do you spend most of your time doing when you have your marketing hat on?*

Planning and analysing.

Meet Online Marketing in Galway
Maricka Burke Keogh | Founder | Ireland

Maricka is the Digital Marketing Manager at IMS Marketing and founder of Online Marketing in Galway (OMiG), a business network for in the West of Ireland. Maricka was winner of JCI Galway 'The Outstanding Young Person of the Year Award' in 2013. She went on to create the OMIG awards in 2014 and the OMIG Digital Summit in 2015.

Question 1: *What are your top marketing words?*

- Inbound
- Strategy
- Digital
- Metrics

Question 2: *What are the key ingredients for a successful marketing campaign?*

Research, measurement, testing, strategy, innovation and creativity.

Question 3: What is your top tip for marketing?

Start your plans afresh, whilst templates can help guide you do not get hung up on having to fit things under certain headings in your plan. Do your homework! Research is important but there comes a stage where you just have to take that leap.

Question 4: *What's your advice to somebody starting a career in marketing?*

Experience is key. Make sure during your early days that you put yourself out there: volunteer, intern or join a society. Build on the skills you will need in your future career.

Question 5: *What do you spend most of your time doing when you have your marketing hat on?*

Reading. I read. I read newspapers, I read blogs, I read books and interesting articles on the topics of marketing, branding and digital marketing.

Meet Congregation.ie
Eoin Kennedy | Founder | Ireland

Eoin Kennedy is a freelance communications executive and entrepreneur based in the west of Ireland. He is the founder of the social media '*unconference*' conference called Congregation. Eoin has co-founded two Internet start ups and is a veteran of the communications industry. He also lectures in social media for the DMI and the Irish Internet Association.

Question 1: *What are your top marketing words?*

- Research
- Investigate
- Plan
- Implement
- Measure
- Experiment
-

Question 2: *What are the key ingredients for a successful marketing campaign?*

Creativity combined with strong delivery/execution against measurable returns.

Question 3: *What is your top tip for marketing?*

Know your customer base and keep asking yourself: *Why am I doing this?*

Question 4: *What's your advice to somebody starting a career in marketing?*

Publish your thoughts. Read as much as you can, connect with people online and demonstrate your ability through creating great content. Don't be afraid to experiment and try something new or ground breaking.

Question 5: *What do you spend most of your time doing when you have your marketing hat on?*

Looking at trends, learning and uncovering new possibilities.

Meet Local Heroes
Paul Fallon | Co- Founder | USA

Paul grew up in B2B software sales, but most recently Co-Founded Local Heroes, a marketplace that connects travelers and locals for authentic experiences.

Question 1: *What are your top marketing words?*

In startup mode, mostly we follow Dave McClure's metrics: **AARRR**. Everything we do is focused on acquiring users and bringing them through the funnel to get to a point where we create enough value that we can extract revenue.

- A - Acquisition
- A - Activation
- R - Retention
- R - Referral
- R - Revenue

Question 2: *What are the key ingredients for a successful marketing campaign?*

Conversion is everything for us. For a large brand awareness is important, but for a young company getting a person to become a user is everything. Then we monitor continuous engagement.

Question 3: *What is your top tip for marketing?*

Watch the metrics, spend marketing budget where the numbers tell you to.

Question 4: *What's your advice to somebody starting a career in marketing?*

Make sure your product team is delivering on your customer promises.

Question 5: *What do you spend most of your time doing when you have your marketing hat on?*

Thinking about messaging and who will best react to what our messaging is.

Meet The McWilliam Park Hotel
David Glynn | Marketing Manager | Ireland

David is responsible for all aspects of marketing in the McWilliam Park Hotel including traditional, online and social. The hotel is located in Co Mayo in the west of Ireland and as been renowned for it's clever national marketing campaigns. David is also an active member of Online Marketing in Galway and is a co-founder of OMiG Digital Summit.

Question 1: *What are your top marketing words?*

Know your customer segments and send marketing messages that are only relevant to them.

Question 2: *What are the key ingredients for a successful marketing campaign?*

Decide on your budget and stick to it. Where are your prospective customers gathering and be present at this stage It could be an event or exhibition or online.

Question 3: *What is your top tip for marketing?*

I think you have to be creative with your ideas and tuned into what is happening locally and nationally. Listen to your customers & especially your staff as they are in the front line and dealing with your customers every minute of every day.

Question 4: *What's your advice to somebody starting a career in marketing?*

With the internet and social media it has never been easier to connect with people. You can easily connect and read the thoughts of top marketing experts.

Question 5: *What do you spend most of your time doing when you have your marketing hat on?*

I am constantly researching and thinking of new campaigns. The ideas happen at the strangest times and places.

Meet Radio Nova
Kevin Branigan | CEO | Ireland

Kevin launched Radio Nova into a very crowded market place in 2010 and has rapidly earned its stripes as one of the most successful arrivals to the airwaves. Broadcasting to Dublin city, county and commuter belt, the station employs a team of almost 40 people.

Question 1: *What are your top marketing words?*

- Seriously
- Additive
- Music

Question 2: *What are the key ingredients for a successful marketing campaign?*

- Simplicity
- Clarity

Question 3: *What is your top tip for marketing?*

Know whom you're trying to target. Don't overcomplicate the message and don't design by committee.

Question 4: *What's your advice to somebody starting a career in marketing?*

Spend some time looking at the Top 100 marketing campaigns EVER on the Internet and try to understand what made them so good. If you don't get it, don't go into marketing!

Question 5: *What do you spend most of your time doing when you have your marketing hat on?*

Admiring good creative, simple advertising campaigns and thinking how I can further hone our brand message.

Meet Biz Growth Media
Krishna De | Author & CEO | Ireland

Krishna is a digital communications and content marketing speaker, commentator, educator and mentor. She works with companies to guide them in how to integrate digital technologies to increase the effectiveness of their external and internal communications, crisis management processes and online reputation management.

Question 1: *What are your top marketing words?*

- Research
- Integrate
- Measure

Question 2: *What are the key ingredients for a successful marketing campaign?*

In today's interactive world the essential good practices are still critical - know your business objectives, thoroughly understand your target audience, have a compelling proposition and manage, measure and monitor your campaign effectiveness so you can course-correct and adjust it to optimise your success.

There are two new ingredients that I would add to the mix for creating marketing success today versus 10 years ago. The first is the increased importance of engaging visual content which is essential if you want to attract coverage from traditional and online media and increase shares (in other words, word of mouth referrals) online. The second is the increased importance of creative campaigns. What may have seemed an innovative idea a year ago can often be quickly copied by others, so it is critical that keep your marketing campaigns fresh and relevant.

Question 3: *What is your top tip for marketing?*

Be prepared to experiment and continue to invest in enhancing your organisations marketing effectiveness and capabilities, and unless you plan to outsource your marketing, embed those skills into your organisation, especially as digital marketing is becoming an essential element of all marketeers skill sets and it is a field that is constantly evolving.

Question 4: *What's your advice to somebody starting a career in marketing?*

Look for opportunities to put your theoretical knowledge into practice and proactively manage your personal brand online and your digital footprint.

Question 5: *What do you spend most of your time doing when you have your marketing hat on?*

Experimenting and researching new approaches, tools and technologies, which will enable to me to support my clients with their marketing and communication goals.

Meet Pocket Anatomy
Thomas King | Marketing Director | Ireland

Thomas oversees all aspects of product development strategy, marketing, PR, liaising with customers worldwide to ensure product fit and also sourcing collaborative partners and investors. Pocket Anatomy's award-winning 3D visual software solution is the Google Earth for healthcare, facilitating doctor-patient diagnoses and communication alongside promoting patient well-being and personal healthcare understanding. Used by over 250,000 people worldwide The company have won many awards for their innovative user-centric design and usability, most recently the 2014 they won Best Tech Startup at BOOST in Amsterdam.

Question 1: *What are your top marketing words?*

- Focus
- Communication
- Alignment

Question 2: *What are the key ingredients for a successful marketing campaign?*

It is vital to know who your target audience is, where they are based (geographically, demographically, online vs offline) and then figure out how best to reach them. Quality metrics and analytics for assessing the results and feedback from any campaign are also very important. You must be able to quantify the relative success of the various components of your campaign and use this knowledge to adjust the mix of your strategy going forward.

Question 3: *What is your top tip for marketing?*

Put yourself in the shoes of your customer. In order to reach, communicate and understand them, you must think like them.

Question 4: *What's your advice to somebody starting a career in marketing?*

Find your own unique voice and bring passion to what you do. Look for inspiration from a wide variety of sources both from within and outside of your own particular industry. If you have a new idea, make a small test, and do so before spending a fortune on the project. By engaging in direct contact with your customers, you will often find out quickly and cheaply if you are on the right track. Get up from your desk! Some of my best creative thoughts arrive when I'm out for a run or hitting the gym!

Question 5: *What do you spend most of your time doing when you have your marketing hat on?*

A lot of the time is spent engaging with our customers seeing how our products are meeting their needs, establishing any gaps that exist and then working on a strategy to close these gaps. We use focused and unfocused methods (both in-house and with external partners) to find creative solutions to these challenges with aim of surprising and delighting our clients. Remember, under-promise and over-deliver and not the reverse!

Meet GroupM
Jonathan Cloonan | Director of Business Development | U.S.A

Jonathan works at GroupM, which is the media investment management arm of WPP, the world's largest marketing communications company. Jonathan was named Forbes '30 Under 30' and works with VICE and GroupM Entertainment in NY and LA. GroupM looks after media spend and content creation for the world's largest brands like Unilever, Nestle, Nike, American Express via their agencies Mindshare, Mediacom, MEC and Maxus.

Question 1: *What are your top marketing words?*

Brands should always respect consumers. In any communications, be real, be authentic and be sincere.

Question 2: *What are the key ingredients for a successful marketing campaign?*

Finding a true and rich consumer insight from which the creative can flow. An insight that genuinely spans a consumer truth, a brand truth and a cultural truth leads to good work. Always.

Question 3: *What is your top tip for marketing?*

Yes, be aware of the latest tech, digital, social trends, gimmicks and fads. But never, ever forget that consumers are human beings with deeply entrenched motivations. Figure out how to satisfy those basic needs and wants better than your competitors and you will win. And make sure that you can communicate your true value proposition, in light of these motivations, better than your competitive set.

Question 4: *What's your advice to somebody starting a career in marketing?*

Live life away from textbooks. Travel, sample other cultures, be curious about new things, follow the Arts, take up an instrument, figure out how to code.... anything that will allow you to bring a unique perspective will add value to your teams and, ultimately, to the marketing communications behind the brands.

Question 5: *What do you spend most of your time doing when you have your marketing hat on?*

I spend most of my time doing two things.

1. Talking to consumers. Listening to them. Understanding their needs, wants, desires, motivations, values, attitudes. Without this deep insight, it's a risk whether a campaign will work or not.

2. Learning about new media, breaking tech trends and identifying whom the hottest start-ups are in the marketplace. I need to advise my clients where to direct their spend and budgets. To do so, I make sure I'm totally up to date on the digital landscape.

Meet Press Play Presentations
Lottie Hearn | Managing Directer | Ireland

Lottie Hearn is a video coach empowering her clients with confidence on camera. With over 20 years of expertise from stage to screen, presenting with impact, Lottie has trained successful individuals, professionals, speakers, TV and video presenters around the globe.

Question 1: *What are your top marketing words?*

- Confidence
- Credibility
- Charisma
- Connection

Learn to be Flawsome – stuff up with confidence, and get over it! Possibilities are only out there, because somebody has the guts to dream them.

Question 2: *What are the key ingredients for a successful marketing campaign?*

In relation to the video element of your campaign:

- Always have a clear video plan – know what every video is specifically for?
- Always include a 'Call to Action' at the end. Help us help you - tell us what you want us to do/ say/ feel/ share with the world after watching?
- Make sure that YOU are your number one production value when filming DIY videos. Make the effort to present the best you on camera that you can.
- Test your lighting and sound to make sure they are the best they can be at that moment and test it, test it, test it, until it works.
- Remember you are the expert in your field, so make us believe in you. If it all goes wrong, just film it again!
- It's OK to keep your video marketing simple – chat to us, tell us why, how and what you offer or do? You don't have to blow thousands on bells and whistles, whizz-bang TV style video ads to promote your 'thang' – you can simply tell us. As long as you let us know what's in it for us as the viewer.

A successful video campaign holds the focus on the only things I care about as I watch you:

- Why should I bother?
- What can you do for me?
- How will you help ease my pain or make my life easier/ better/ richer when I buy into brand you?

Question 3: *What is your top tip for marketing?*

Use video. People buy from people they like, trust and believe in. Video is about connecting to real people in a real way, so video scripts need to be a conversation chat, not a website text monologue. Say it how you'd say it face to face, not how you'd write it and connect through the camera lens, as if I'm really there with you. You're allowed to enjoy it too! Look and sound like you mean it and always keep going through to the end – you're perceived 'stuff up' might be the best, most fun, super-great video you do!

Question 4: *What's your advice to somebody starting a career in marketing?*

Have fun with it. Business doesn't have to be so serious. It just has to be true.

Question 5: *What do you spend most of your time doing when you have your marketing hat on?*

Video! - Finding ways to help others who work with me. I love promoting other people's videos and success using all sorts of social media, as it's not always about my own videos or just what I do. I know so many other people have fantastic, amazing, brilliant information, knowledge and skills to share too and when they do that via video – it's a great thing for me to be able to pass that on, spreading the word and sharing the love! As a video coach, professional speaker and co-preneur, I value mutually beneficial collaborations and being part of the sharing culture that's on the rise today.

Meet Snap

Ronan Walsh | Business Development Manager | Ireland

Ronan is a business and networking enthusiast with vast experience in sales and marketing across a wide spectrum of industry sectors. Ronan has a love for creative marketing and developing brand awareness. Ronan is also the founder of My Toys Direct, President of JCI Galway and co-founder of the Sales Master Minders.

Question 1: *What are your top marketing words?*

Marketing has to be personal and offer consumers value. Your customers see so much advertising every day that it is so important that you have a clear message and build a strong brand.

Question 2: *What are the key ingredients for a successful marketing campaign?*

Specific calls to action, bright clear messages that appeal to your customer base. Give the right message to the right people through the right marketing channels. And most importantly of all, don't be afraid to think outside the box - be different, be memorable.

Question 3: *What is your top tip for marketing?*

Whether is traditional or digital marketing, you need to be consistent. Develop a 'voice' for your brand that appeals to and fits your customer base.

Question 4: *What's your advice to somebody starting a career in marketing?*

Stick to your beliefs. Don't be afraid to stand up and speak when you have an idea or don't agree with something. Offer your suggestions and always be **creative**!

Question 5: *What do you spend most of your time doing when you have your marketing hat on?*

Always starts with a pen and a blank page. Scribbling ideas then mapping them together to create a strategy and a plan on how to deliver the message at hand.

Meet Nua Naturals
Hilary Foley | CEO | Ireland

Hilary is the force behind NUA Naturals, an organic health food company located in the west of Ireland serving the UK and European markets. The company is situated at the cutting edge of emerging global trends such as Gluten Free, Raw and Organic.

Question 1: *What are your top marketing words?*

Social Media is vital to our success and needs **continuous investment** in both time and money. It is an essential platform to engage directly with your consumers. A small investment of a few euros and an hour a day can see your brand awareness to potential consumers grow, online sales soar and brand engagement increase dramatically.

Question 2: *What are the key ingredients for a successful marketing campaign?*

Monitor, monitor, monitor! If you do not see what is working well or rather failing to work, then you cannot move forward with a successful campaign.

Question 3: *What is your top tip for marketing?*

Continuous market research is essential. By continuously assessing the industry, consumers and competitors, it will enable a company to gain a serious competitive edge.

Question 4: *What's your advice to somebody starting a career in marketing?*

Experience is essential. Whether it is asking to help run a local charity's social media or helping out a new start-up company on a part time basis, experience is vital. Being able to **adapt** to a new industry will be the key to your success.

Question 5: *What do you spend most of your time doing when you have your marketing hat on?*

Monitoring the competition and spotting new trends. Always keep and eye on what your competitors are doing and make sure you do everything better than them.

Meet Lacreme Barcelona
Irene Gracia Delgado | Creator and CEO | Spain

Irene is an expert in naturopathy and kinesiology. With her knowledge in natural remedies and the functioning of the human body, Irene has created therapeutic formulas for every skin type. She has created a bespoke product line and designed a successful cosmetic brand called Lacreme Barcelona.

Question 1: *What are your top marketing words?*

- Customers
- Therapeutic
- Natural
- Vintage

Question 2: *What are the key ingredients for a successful marketing campaign?*

The key ingredients to a successful campaign is to learn what people are looking for and show them you have what they need to get better quality in their lives. Be clear about what kind of people you want to sell to and get the aesthetics and image right so that you can communicate in their language.

Question 3: *What is your top tip for marketing?*

Sell a lifestyle, not just a product.

Question 4: *What's your advice to somebody starting a career in marketing?*

Understand consumers and consumer behaviour.

Question 5: *What do you spend most of your time doing when you have your marketing hat on?*

Taking photographs, being creative, writing text and emotionally charged messages to deliver. Learning about other products similar to mine. Researching the market in which I want to sell. Learning more about my competition. Collaborating with other young entrepreneurs.

Meet InmoXara
Gema Garcia | Marketing Director | Ireland

InmoXara is a small family owned real estate agency. Gemma is a lover of marketing and relationships. Since its inception, InmoXara has grown gradually and is one of Spain's leading referral and estate agencies.

Question 1: *What are your top marketing words?*

Always try to convey **transparency, confidence** and **security** for all parties in the purchase process. Make the sale of the product a pleasant experience where the customer feels informed at all times. One of the slogans we use most is: '*I speak clearly.*'

Question 2: *What are the key ingredients for a successful marketing campaign?*

A good marketing campaign should **add value**. Before you start a campaign, the most important aspect is to design a good marketing plan, taking into account the market you will target. Make sure that both the online and the offline campaign compliment each other. Follow the same script.

Question 3: *What is your top tip for marketing?*

Investigate, keep up, know in detail your sector and study your competition. Discuss in detail your campaigns and see what works. Try to innovate and be different.

Question 4: *What's your advice to somebody starting a career in marketing?*

Clearly define your brand and make your mark with content marketing. The best content is one that is transparent and clear.

Question 5: *What do you spend most of your time doing when you have your marketing hat on?*

Making the most of my resources by creating engaging campaigns that convey good positive feelings for our potential customer.

Meet Cava Recaredo

Alex Bautista | Sales and Marketing Manager | Spain

Alex Bautista is the international sales and marketing manager for a small boutique winery based in Barcelona. Recaredo is an acclaimed best cava producer in Spain and can be found in the top restaurants throughout the world. They are operational in 35 countries.

Question 1: *What are your top marketing words?*

Certainty – Believe – Honesty - Trust

Question 2: *What are the key ingredients for a successful marketing campaign?*

Resolution and focused: Be practical, knowing what you want and what you are going to get, and if it makes sense with the resources you have. Get everyone with a clear idea of the goals and results.
Timing: Pick the right time and organise the campaign work so you can achieve it on time.
Believe: Get everyone involved in the campaign to believe, so they are certain about the results to obtain.
Encourage: Encourage everyone involved to excel and take ownership. Make them part of it. Sharing is caring.

Question 3: *What is your top tip for marketing?*

Have a clear idea where you want your business to be in. **Think BIG** and believe! Scrub, analyse and get as much information as possible.

Question 4: *What's your advice to somebody starting a career in marketing?*

Work-hard, be patience and most of all be ready for a wonderful journey and a lot of excitement.

Question 5: *What do you spend most of your time doing when you have your marketing hat on?*

I am thinking of the best opportunities to make our brand even more exposed to the right audience in the most effective way.

Meet Heineken Ireland
John Kelly | Off Trade Director | Ireland

A graduate of UCC with a BSc in Food Business and a postgraduate Diploma in marketing from the Smurfit School of Business, John has held a number of senior positions in FMCG over the past 20 years. As Off Trade Director for Heineken Ireland, John has led a strategy and vision culminating in Heineken Ireland winning the top lager supplier in Ireland and the Heineken Brand becoming the top Irish alcohol brand in the recent 2014 Checkout Top Brands listing.

Question 1: *What are your top marketing words?*

Know your consumer and shopper intimately. Listen to understand them. Speak their language, but always with **authenticity**.

Question 2: *What are the key ingredients for a successful marketing campaign?*

Understand the brief, what is the objective of the campaign? To be disruptive, build awareness, incite to purchase etc. Once established understand the best channels to speak with your target consumer: social media, print, outdoor, etc.

Question 3: *What is your top tip for marketing?*

See answer to question one! And always remember, if marketing isn't either brand equity building or driving incremental sales, it's not worth doing.

Question 4: *What's your advice to somebody starting a career in marketing?*

Get into trade, understand the customer, your route to market and the trade. Speak and listen to your consumer and **know your return on investment** on every euro of your marketing investment.

Question 5: *What do you spend most of your time doing when you have your marketing hat on?*

Innovation. Innovation and more... **Innovation**. This is the life-blood of any organisation no matter what size.

Meet Creva Agri International
Noel Kelly | CEO | Ireland

Noel is an award winning international marketer who firmly believes that forging solid life long business partnerships is the route to great sales. Noel has facilitated B2B relationships across the globe for over 12 years. An accomplished Dairy & 'Sales' Farmer, Noel is an owner in two companies which have both witnessed triple digit growth in the last 4 years.

Question 1: *What are your top marketing words?*

- Investigate
- Brand equity
- Customer confidence
- Market a solution

Question 2: *What are the key ingredients for a successful marketing campaign?*

- Always **think**: Before, during and after.
- Get your **message** across; give confidence to targeted customers.
- **Quantify** your **results**.
- Have a MIGHTY **call to action**!

Question 3: What is your top tip for marketing?

Be clear in your objectives. Understand customer's needs to gain their interest. **Push the boundaries of innovation** and **grab the early adopters**.

Question 4: *What's your advice to somebody starting a career in marketing?*

Be confident in your product/service. Don't be afraid to get your hands dirty! Do as they do, see as they see!

Question 5: *What do you spend most of your time doing when you have your marketing hat on?*

Thinking, rethinking and analysing. Brainstorming ideas on a mind map. Believe that a great marketing idea can come to you at any time and always have a means to capture it.

Meet Cloud Computing
Tim Pullen | Managing Director| Ireland

Tim is a sales and delivery focused business director with extensive experience of building and leading successful teams. Supplying technical and business project resources, Cloud Consulting Ltd are one of Ireland's leading cloud technology consultancies with 5 years of continuous business growth with revenues doubling each year.

Question 1: *What are your top marketing words?*

Quality, Quality & Quality

Question 2: *What are the key ingredients for a successful marketing campaign?*

- Relevant, topical and personalised messaging
- Never underestimate the power of humour
- Quality (clean) data
- Rapid response times – never let the contact get cold
- A relentless belief that you are the best

Question 3: *What is your top tip for marketing?*

Never accept second best – always go for the best that you can afford and let others think 'I wish I had done that…'

Question 4: *What's your advice to somebody starting a career in marketing?*

It is not a career – **marketing is a way of life**. You have to believe that you can change the world.

Question 5: *What do you spend most of your time doing when you have your marketing hat on?*

Arguing with the marketing team! Why can't we do it that way?

Meet Salesforce
Mark Stanley | VP of Digital Marketing and Marketing Operations | Europe

Mark Stanley is VP of digital marketing and marketing operations for Salesforce.com in Europe. Salesforce.com is the #1 CRM platform and the leader in sales, service, marketing and cloud platforms worldwide. Mark has been with salesforce.com since 2000 and leads a team of digital marketing professionals across Europe.

Question 1: *What are your top marketing words?*

- Trial
- Demo
- Success
- #1
- Powerful

Question 2: *What are the key ingredients for a successful marketing campaign?*

A marketing campaign should be very targeted in its objective so that everyone is clear on whether it has been a success after the fact. It should have a topical theme so that prospects connect it to current trends, **have amazing copy and creative to convey the message clearly**, put existing successful customers at the centre as proof of the benefits of adopting the product or service in question, and have a clear and compelling call to action to capture interest. Finally, ensure your sales team are fully briefed on everything related to your campaign and are incentivised to track any leads and sales generated in your CRM system. This helps you measure the impact of your campaign, meaning you can see whether or not it was successful.

Question 3: *What is your top tip for marketing?*

Experiment, measure, optimise. Try new things - set aside 10 percent of your budget to experiment with a new channel or campaign. Then measure its impact. In a world where more advertising budget is moving towards online and mobile platforms, our ability to measure the impact of our marketing campaigns is increasing. That's a dream to any marketer as it provides **visibility** into the **impact** of what we do, allowing us to be more successful. Ensure you have the tools to measure the channels and campaigns you manage - website, email, social media, PPC - there is a measurement tool for everything and many are free to use. Once you can measure, you can optimise towards a certain goal whether that be social followers, social engagement, email clicks, website visits, leads or sales generated.

Question 4: *What's your advice to somebody starting a career in marketing?*

Understand the numbers. What are your goals, and how are you doing against those goals in detail throughout the funnel? A marketing role today is much more about creative execution; it's about being business focused and understanding the impact of your work and how to optimise your results further with your limited resources. Be a close partner to your management team and sales teams by understanding the numbers and how you are helping grow your business. You will thank me for it some day.

Question 5: *What do you spend most of your time doing when you have your marketing hat on?*

As above, I'm looking at the trends in our data. What's performing well that we can scale up, what's not working that we need to focus on, how does our performance in one country, segment, channel compare against another? Outside of that, looking at what are our competitors or world leaders in other industries doing in their marketing that we can learn from. Whilst salesforce.com is the most innovative company in the world for three years running according to Forbes magazine, we also don't have exclusivity on good ideas.

Meet IMS Marketing
Kevin Moran | Founder and Managing Director | Ireland

Kevin Moran is founder ofMarketing, a full service-marketing agency established in 2007. Prior to this, Kevin held senior sales and marketing roles with Irish SMEs and multinationals and in 2004 was awarded 'International Marketing Person of the Year' in Ireland. Kevin is a strategic advisor for a number of State agencies.

Question 1: *What are your top marketing words?*

- Focus
- Customer understanding
- Positioning

Question 2: *What are the key ingredients for a successful marketing campaign?*

- Senior management buy-in is key
- Clear objectives are essential
- Measurement from as early as possible

Question 3: *What is your top tip for marketing?*

Define your strategy and align everything around this. Always seek to understand and refine your **value proposition** within this strategy.

Question 4: *What's your advice to somebody starting a career in marketing?*

Get out from behind the desk and get an understanding of your customer, competitors and marketplace.

Question 5: *What do you spend most of your time doing when you have your marketing hat on?*

I am planning. I am focused on my customers, meeting my customers and learning about the needs of my customers.

Meet European Business Awards
Adrian Tripp | CEO | UK

Adrian Tripp is CEO and founder of the European Business Awards, Europe's biggest and most prestigious business competition. Adrian previously built and sold Quest Media, a highly regarded business publisher. He also runs Tracc Films, a fast growing corporate film making company with operations in the UK, US and India.

Question 1: *What are your top marketing words?*

Return on Investment and Results

Question 2: *What are the key ingredients for a successful marketing campaign?*

Answer the following questions:

- What's the objective?
- What is in it for your audience?
- How are you going to reach them?
- How are you going to get their attention?
- How are you going to get them to think or do something different after exposure to your messaging/campaign?
- How are you going to measure the results?

Question 3: *What is your top tip for marketing?*

Educate - use video and make 'how to' and demo films.

Question 4: *What's your advice to somebody starting a career in marketing?*

Think digital.

Question 5: *What do you spend most of your time doing when you have your marketing hat on?*

Sitting in the shoes of our present and future customers and trying to understand what they want and how we can best deliver that for them.

Meet The Irish Academy of Public Relations
Ellen Gunning | Director | Ireland

Ellen Gunning formed the Irish Academy of Public Relations in 1992. The Academy specialises in communications training. Online courses in public relations, print journalism, event management, marketing, radio journalism and grammar are taught worldwide. The Academy has graduates in 32 countries and teaches PR online in five languages. Partner colleges in Ireland, Greece and Nigeria also teach the courses.

Question 1: *What are your top marketing words?*

Use a bow and arrow - not a splurge gun!

Question 2: *What are the key ingredients for a successful marketing campaign?*

Know your target market - where they live, what they read, who they listen to. The more you know, the better you can target them.
Give them information, which is relevant to their needs - nothing else.
Prime the market with stories, photos, blogs and media coverage in advance of a new sales drive.

Question 3: *What is your top tip for marketing?*

Think long and hard about what you commit your money to. If you choose the wrong vehicle your money is wasted.

Question 4: *What's your advice to somebody starting a career in marketing?*

Get as much experience as possible initially - try everything. Find what you like (which will also be the area you are good at) and then decide where to specialise.

Question 5: *What do you spend most of your time doing when you have your marketing hat on?*

Because we market our courses internationally, most of my time is spent trying to understand the different cultures, languages, influencers and, particularly, the different styles of communication in each country.

Meet La Tagliatella
Fernando Olivares | Global Marketing Director | Spain

Fernando leads La Tagliatella marketing efforts with an experience of over 12 years in the area of marketing of different retail and hospitality businesses. La Tagliatella is the leader in the Italian Restaurant chain sector in Spain. In recent years it has begun a process of international expansion by opening stores in the United States, France, Germany and China.

Question 1: *What are your top marketing words?*

- Customer satisfaction
- Brand

Question 2: *What are the key ingredients for a successful marketing campaign?*

- Having a clear objective aligned with company strategy.
- Choose a simple idea, yet powerful and direct communication.
- Select the appropriate media mix to target objective, investment capacity and characteristics of content to communicate.
- Keep your personality and tone of voice coherent and consistent.
- Cook all ingredients with passion and drops of creativity.
- Measure, measure and measure the results to adjust the recipe.

Question 3: *What is your top tip for marketing?*

It is more important to engage in satisfying and retaining than to worry about attracting new customers when existing customers are not happy.

Question 4: *What is your advice to someone starting a career in marketing?*

Always be curious, do not stop learning and be suspicious of anyone who tells you they are an expert.

Question 5: *What do you spend most of your time doing when you have your marketing hat on?*

Marketing! It's the only hat I wear!

Meet KFC/AmRest Spain
Gema Rey Calvo | Marketing Manager | Spain

Gema brings more than 12 years experience in marketing departments in different sectors such as banking, pharmaceutical and retail to KFC Spain. They are part of the Amrest group, which is the biggest restaurant operator in Europe with 31 KFC restaurants in Spain. With 7 years working at KFC, Gema has been focused on developing and activating the point of sales through local store marketing, managing value proposals, looking for profitability and increasing brand image and collaborating with the franchisor: Yum! Restaurants.

Question 1: *What are the main words in marketing?*

Marketing is **common sense**, that's all...

Question 2: *What are the key ingredients for a successful marketing campaign?*

You must **know your client** and also highlight the main benefit of the product.

Question 3: *What is your best advice on marketing?*

Adapt yourself or die. You must **adapt yourself** to the macroeconomic environment, new laws, new trend on the market and new habits of your target market.

Question 4: *What is your advice to someone starting a career in marketing?*

Keep your eyes and your ears so opened, not only to catch everything around you for your colleagues, but to know new trends. Keep an eye on your main competitors or other businesses in the sector.

Question 5: *What occupies most of your time when you put your hat marketer?*

Analysing data and the results of the actions and campaigns. Sometimes also spying on the competition!

Meet The Zip Yard
Caroline Wallace | Marketing Director | Ireland

Caroline is responibile for the branding and marketing of The Zip Yard, an alterations boutique. The company has evolved into a modern retail business specialising in not only alterations, but restyling & remodelling of bespoke and quality garments.

Question 1: *What are your top marketing words?*

Recession proof, on trend, remodelling, restyling, boutique, modern, high street, contemporary, quick turnaround, express service, customer service.

Question 2: *What are the key ingredients for a successful marketing campaign?*

- **Preparation**: A clear strategy must be defined & a schedule created that must be followed.
- **Promotion**: The necessary mediums for advertising must be defined: Print, TV, Radio and Social Media.
- **Sexy**: Visual images & catchy colourful use of photos, text, language and sounds.
- **All**: Everyone must commit to the same objective and row the boat together.

Question 3: *What is your top tip for marketing?*

Prepare, promote & present like it is your one and only opportunity.

Question 4: *What's your advice to somebody starting a career in marketing?*

Keep abreast of current and progressing trends such as social media, video marketing etc. Marketing like technology is only as good as the most popular ideas. **Have the ability to bend.**

Question 5: *What do you spend most of your time doing when you have your marketing hat on?*

Repeating the actions. Reinforcing the notion. One ad is nothing, one editorial is nothing, one social media post is nothing. The message must be scheduled for repeat, otherwise it will be forgotten.

Meet Escape Goats
Sean Bushell | CEO | Ireland

Sean Bushell has a background in journalism, media and events. He is CEO & Founder of Irish based start up: Escape Goats. The new platform matches the user to great activities and providers in real time.

Question 1: *What are your top marketing words?*

Superior customer experience.

Question 2: *What are the key ingredients for a successful marketing campaign?*

Show that you are solving a problem, or offering a very positive experience.

Question 3: *What is your top tip for marketing?*

Talk about the benefits, not the features. Show exactly the positive impact your product or service will have on their lives.

Question 4: *What's your advice to somebody starting a career in marketing?*

Listen to your customer. Sometimes the user won't know what they're looking for, but if you listen to the challenges they face, you can discover the solution. As Henry Ford said, *'If I had asked people what they wanted, they would have said faster horses.'* I believe that in all aspects of life, you get what you're willing to accept, so **celebrate the small victories**, get back up after the setbacks and always keep moving forward.

Question 5: *What do you spend most of your time doing when you have your marketing hat on?*

I listen to the experiences of potential Escape Goats users looking for something to do and explore how we can make theirs a better experience. I also talk to lots of people who are smarter than me about what we're trying to do at Escape Goats - we are always learning.

Meet Velocity Bike Store
Mark Mc Keigue | CEO | Ireland

Mark is CEO of Velocity Bike Store, a high end bike and triathlon retail Store in Ireland and also TURAS Bikes, the first Irish high end bike brand. Combining his attention to detail derived from a background in 5 star hotel management and extensive end user experience within the bike and triathlon area, Mark offers an extensive solution based expertise to the bike and triathlon industry.

Question 1: *What are your top marketing words?*

Listen, listen, listen and **LISTEN**!

Question 2: *What are the key ingredients for a successful marketing campaign?*

I think the key ingredient in a successful marketing campaign is content. It must be of value to the audience. Be that entertainment value, informational value or value of another type. There must be something in it for the audience to get them truly engaged.

Question 3: *What is your top tip for marketing?*

Marketing is about listening to your customers not speaking 'at' them. The content is about encouraging the audience to share their thoughts.

Question 4: *What's your advice to somebody starting a career in marketing?*

Read this book!!!! And be prepared to continuously learn. Marketing is a game in which the rules constantly change.

Question 5: *What do you spend most of your time doing when you have your marketing hat on?*

Coming up with content that is both engaging and of value to my audience. I also spend a considerable time trying to find ways to test approaches and measure results of our efforts because it must be measured and there must be a way to quantify the marketing spend.

Meet Virtual Office Worx
Jenny Brennan | CEO | Ireland

In 2011 Jenny Brennan set-up a virtual assistant business to provide businesses with outsourced social media support solutions to save owners time and help them increase sales. As her own business developed and grew online Jenny became passionate about connecting with like-minded business people & industry influencers on social media to grow her business and now helps her clients to do the same. As a result, Jenny has had the opportunity to work with influencers in her field including Ian Cleary of Razor Social, Emeric Ernoult of AgoraPulse and, more recently, Jon Loomer, the world's leading Facebook marketing expert for advanced Facebook Marketers.

Question 1: *What are your top marketing words?*

- Real results
- Proven
- Value
- Credible

Question 2: *What are the key ingredients for a successful marketing campaign?*

Proper segmentation of prospects, strong product offering, stellar content, strategic goal plan with actionable tasks that lead to desired outcomes.

Question 3: *What is your top tip for marketing?*

Be Human!

Question 4: *What's your advice to somebody starting a career in marketing?*

Stay with it, know that change is definite and have a willingness to **be flexible**.

Question 5: *What do you spend most of your time doing when you have your marketing hat on?*

Listening to what people are saying.

Meet Sage
Andy Penfold | Head of Marketing | UK

Andy has 25 years experience in European B2B marketing roles within hardware, software and distribution and leads the marketing team for Sage UK and Ireland's small to medium size business segment.

Question 1: *What are your top marketing words?*

FREE SELL NOW

Free = cost to the customer
Sell = value to the customer
Now = delivery to the customer

Question 2: *What are the key ingredients for a successful marketing campaign?*

Marry above principles with insight, targets and targeting.

Question 3: *What is your top tip for marketing?*

Measurement = learning = improvement

Question 4: *What's your advice to somebody starting a career in marketing?*

First of all, good choice, it is a great career option. Look for variety; be prepared to ditch everything at the last minute as the market/budget/competition changes the landscape. Marketing is an 'Arts' subject but apply scientific principles to develop, assess, learn, measure and improve.

Question 5: *What do you spend most of your time doing when you have your marketing hat on?*

I question my colleagues, my team and myself to find out how we can get better.

Meet Obeo

Kate Cronin | Designer and Co-Founder | Ireland

Kate is lead designer and co-founder of Obeo. They have created a fuss-free recycling solution that helps people to help their environment. Their first product is a compostable box for food waste recycling. The Obeo food waste box currently retails in over 170 stores in Ireland as well as online.

Question 1*: What are your top marketing words?*

- Customer focused
- Story-based
- Social
- Community driven

Question 2*: What are the key ingredients for a successful marketing campaign?*

A customer focused campaign with coordinated execution and continuous monitoring and tweaking.

Question 3*: What is your top tip for marketing?*

Put yourself in your customer's shoes. It's not about preaching to them, it's about listening to them. Generate customer profiles and refer to them often to see if your message is hitting the mark.

Question 4*: What's your advice to somebody starting a career in marketing?*

You will never be finished learning, get used to that. You can never stop keeping up to date.

Question 5*: What do you spend most of your time doing when you have your marketing hat on?*

Analysing. Analysing sales, website traffic, conversions, social media performance, etc. Checking what's working and what's not.

Meet Pat Divilly Fitness
Pat Divilly | Founder and CEO | Ireland

Pat founded Pat Divilly Fitness in May of 2012 whilst working as a waiter in a pizzeria. He decided he had to give personal training one last chance. He took the €200 he had left to his name to get 5000 flyers printed up advertising a fitness class on his local beach. The first morning he trained 5 people on the beach. Within a year he had opened a studio and was training over 200 clients in it and many more via online training programs. Today, three years on, he is a motivational speaker, best selling author and services 2000 clients monthly via his online training courses and his training studio.

Question 1: *What are your top marketing words?*

I know within my industry I've often heard the word 'marketing' be used with negative connotations attached to it. I learnt early on that whatever industry you are in you are selling and my belief is that if you aren't learning to market yourself and your talents you are doing a disservice to people. The reason I got into the fitness industry initially was to share my passion for training and nutrition. If I wasn't prepared to put myself out there and market, I'd be left with a very small number of people whom I could help. Learning to market effectively using social media now allows me to help thousands all over the world every month.

Question 2: *What are the key ingredients for a successful marketing campaign?*

I think positioning yourself as the expert in your field makes any marketing campaign a lot easier. Becoming an author and presenting seminars all around the country has helped position me as a go-to expert in the health and wellness industry. This has allowed me to build up a strong online following to which I can advertise my services. Instead of having to turn to print media where a tiny fraction of the audience will take interest in my 'ad' I can market to a following that have shown they are already interested in what I provide. As a result my online courses and seminars can sell out in minutes without the need for expensive traditional advertising. I think its important to craft a message that compels the prospect to take action and to deliver it in the media that is most suited to their ideal demographic. For example a company promoting a nightclub are probably going to see a better return in using social media which their clients use all the time instead of sending out newsletters or flyers.

Question 3: *What is your top tip for marketing?*

The message you put across in your marketing needs to be congruent with your service or product. In other words I think you need to be true to yourself and what you are offering. **Honesty and transparency are priceless**. If I advertise a women's weight loss course in a relaxed and fun environment and the customer turns up to a military style boot-camp the message being marketed isn't congruent. I think crafting the right message will attract the client who is the right fit for the product or service.

Question 4: *What's your advice to somebody starting a career in marketing?*

'You can only sell garbage once!' is something that always stuck with me. No matter how good you are at marketing you need to have a quality product or service that people will benefit from. For me **integrity is key**. I want to follow through on any promise I make or benefit I outline in my marketing. Marketing is massively important but I see a lot of people jumping the gun and reading marketing books before they have mastered their craft. As a result they can get the customers but can't retain. It is easier to keep existing customers than it is to go looking for new customers!

Question 5: *What do you spend most of your time doing when you have your marketing hat on?*

I try to step back and look at it from the prospects point of view. I design an 'avatar' of my ideal client. If it is a busy mum who is looking to lose weight I will try to think of the type of roadblocks she has faced in her weight loss journey to date. As part of this I will sometimes survey people from the given demographic. From there I will look to provide a solution to their biggest obstacles and then present testimonials from clients in similar standing who have seen the benefits of my programs. Everyone wants a service that is customised to their goal. I think too many businesses sell what they think people need instead of getting into the mindset of the client and thinking of what it is that they want.

Meet WorkCompass
Alan O'Rourke | Director of Marketing | Ireland

WorkCompass sell online employee performance review and performance management software. An easy and effective solution to manage, develop and engage teams. This is B2B enterprise marketing with long sales cycles.

Question 1: *What are your top marketing words?*

Lead capture, Inbound (Slow to start but cheap and fantastic ROI), Outbound (Fast to start but expensive), Great content (30%), Content promotion (70%) and SEO.

Question 2: *What are the key ingredients for a successful marketing campaign?*

Our approach has always been to be a helpful evergreen resource. From experience we know these types of campaigns get bookmarked, linked to and shared most. They also position us as a thought leader in our industry. The evergreen element is important. This means a resource that never dates. It also means our marketing activities and results get compounded over time. So instead of doing one campaign this month. Stopping it then doing another campaign next month. With evergreen content and resources in month two we have two resource campaigns running, in month 12 we have 12 etc. The ultimate measure of success is capturing an email address. Once we get a prospect into the top of the funnel we do not have to pay to acquire that person again. They might not be ready to buy now but we keep in touch and we will be there when they are.

Question 3: *What is your top tip for marketing?*

Know your numbers. Know how many people you have going into the top of your funnel and how many are closing at the end of the funnel. All your marketing decisions and plans will come from knowing these numbers. Once you have these numbers and they are performing well you will have great leverage to go to your CFO and ask for budget to experiment with more interesting and fun campaigns. If I can slip in a second tip it is to do less but promote it more.

Question 4: *What's your advice to somebody starting a career in marketing?*

Read and try everything. You really need a natural curiosity for this and a certain amount of technical prowess so you can test quickly without waiting on technical resources. In the last 4 companies I have worked in the business models and markets were all very different. The types of marketing that got traction for one business and market would not work in the next. Experience was not the deciding factor in the job, but being curious and being able to solve problems was. You need to look at a market and try out 5-10 different channels to find out what works. Once you get any sort of traction you need to be able to drill deeper into it, test it and work out if the channel is effective enough to be profitable. If it is profitable you need to be able to automate it, grow it and look at the next channel to test. And learn excel... see next answer!

Question 5: *What do you spend most of your time doing when you have your marketing hat on?*

Microsoft Excel or Google spreadsheets - Unfortunately sales and marketing involves so many separate systems that excel is still the only way to pull the data together into a single overview. At the start of every week I am analysing last weeks campaigns and graphing the results. Web and social traffic is measured and goals are analysed to see what channel or piece of content was successful and what wasn't. This data is cross-checked with the sales team to ensure nothing has fallen through the cracks. SEO keywords and traffic is measured to ensure our numbers are growing and the results are what we need. All this is then compiled into a one page marketing report for the teams Tuesday meeting where we compare against previous weeks and decide what we are doing in the week ahead. Even the week ahead is planned in excel with dates and expected results so we can measure it next week.

Meet El Pais
Laura Madera Calle | Brand Manager | Spain

With over 10 years working in Spain's leading newspaper and media outlet El Pais. Laura is the Brand Manager and is responsible for the brand. El Pais has more than 1.7 million readers in print and over 12 million in its web. Laura is a great lover of the theatre and directed her first play, the **critically** acclaimed *'39 Defaults.'* Laura has worked globally overseeing the communications, marketing and production of different shows on both sides of the Atlantic, in New York and Madrid.

Question 1: *What are your top marketing words?*

Imagination – Creativity – Objectives - Knowledge

Question 2: *What are the key ingredients for a successful marketing campaign?*

High product knowledge, the audience to which it is addressed and good creativity that communicates the message you want. Furthermore, **agility and responsiveness** is important for refining your campaign. If something does not work, be able to detect it and improve it.

Question 3: *What is your top tip for marketing?*

Understand the product you sell and the people for whom it's intended. Be creative and do not put limits on your imagination.

Question 4: *What's your advice to somebody starting a career in marketing?*

Be creative. Be able to reinvent yourself. Be self-critical and understand every detail of the product with which you work. **Believe in what you do** and enjoy.

Question 5: *What do you spend most of your time doing when you have your marketing hat on?*

Looking for ways to give a new twist to what we are doing. This can be a return to creative online contests and connecting with our customers on social networks.

Acknowledgements

Thank you to my brothers: Ronan, Parisch and Gene. Thank you to my dad, Ray and my mam, Margaret, to whom I dedicate this book. Also, muchas gracias to my wonderful wife Eva, and my awesome children, Mani and Alana.

Thank you to Niall Killilea, Louise Niemann, Ray McDonnell, James Kent, and all The City Bin Co. staff and customers. A special big thank you to Gene Browne, CEO of The City Bin Co. (and my brother!) for his endless support and belief in me and in my crazy ideas. Thank you to Malek, Anas and all of my averda family. Thank you to Dr. Utlan Sharkey, Eoin Kennedy and Kevin Moran for your input. Thank you Aidan Daly for guiding me with the interview questions, Anne Torres for inviting me to talk about marketing and selling to the leaders of tomorrow, all at J.E. Cairnes School of Business, National University of Ireland, Galway, the NUI Business society and Entrepreneur Society. Thank you Sean Weafer, Eamonn O'Brien, Lottie Hearn and all my colleagues at the Professional Speaking Association. I am so lucky to have such a professional network at my doorstep. Thank you to the fellow co-founders of the Sales Master Minders, Darragh O Connor, Ronan Walsh, Bernie Turley, Sean Quirke and all the members who have inspired me to reach for the stars. Thank you to my good friend, Noel Kelly, for showing me my true value. Thank you to Kevin Fahey and all the members of the Business Leadership Forum. This is a place where I have learned to see and believe in myself.

To my good friend and fellow business enthusiast, Evy Perez for always sharing business ideas and giving encouragement. Thank you for being part of the Spanish journey of the Binman's Guide. Thank you for your friendship, the coffee meetings and the continuous support. Thank you to my Spanish friend Miguel Losada for encouraging and helping me to bring my work to the Spanish mercado! Thank you to all at the Spanish Embassy in Dublin.

Thank you to my editor Dr. Niall McElwee and his team for their attention to detail and professionalism. You are a master of your craft. Thank you Anthony Sloan, Parisch Browne, and Luke O'Donnell (master wordsmith of the world!) for sharing your valued time and generosity in reading, rereading and editing. Thank you Krishna De for writing the beautiful foreword for this book. Thank you to all the business people who gave me their time and wisdom for the interviews.

About the Author

Oisin is passionate about smart selling, metric-focus marketing and providing excellent customer service. An internationally mobile business enthusiast, Oisin works in waste management in Europe and the Middle East.

Oisin's first book *'The Binman's Guide to Selling'* is an Amazon bestseller, and received international praises from top global business experts Marshall Goldsmith, Libby Gill, Verne Harnish, Jeffrey J.Fox, Al Ries and Dr Paddi Lund.

Oisin's intention is to write a series of business books that will guide, motivate and inspire business owners and their teams. This is the second book in the series and will be followed by the 'The Binmans Guide to Customer Service' and many more!

Oisin's business learnings come from his time and experience in one of the most exciting and fastest growing companies in Ireland, The City Bin Co., an award winning utility company based in Ireland. He works for The City Bin Co. as part of the sales, marketing and innovation team. He also built and looks after the company's digital marketing.

Oisin also works as head of key account management for B2B in the UAE for averda, the largest environmental solutions provider in the MENA region. He was involved in implementing the sales process, training the sales team and coaching the key account management team.

Oisin regularly gives keynote talks and workshops to businesses, business groups and business schools on selling, social media marketing, marketing, motivation and customer service. He is a member of The Professional Speaking Association UK & Ireland.

When Oisin is not too busy selling and speaking, he enjoys working and travelling between the UAE, West of Ireland & Spain, where he immerses himself in the rich Spanish culture.

www.oisinbrowne.com